Prepper's Guide to Wealth:
Crypto-Gold-Barter & More

*How Understanding Money Will
Enhance Your Peace of Mind*

By Ron Brown

R&C Publishing

Newark Valley, New York

Published by:
R&C Publishing Company
15 Dr. Knapp Road South
Newark Valley, NY 13811

Table of Contents

Foreword

When it comes to money, the old adage "what you don't know can't hurt you" is wrong. Being oblivious to money, currency, and their sidekick wealth preservation, cannot only hurt you but can jeopardize your ability to have a roof over your head and food on the table.

Fact: The ability to acquire goods and services depends on currency as a medium of exchange for goods and services. But what exactly is currency these days?

Most of us know about fiat money and precious metals but what about digital currency and Bitcoin/cryptocurrency? How does it all work and more important, what role does the Federal government, Federal Reserve aka "The Fed", and the Central Bank play in all this?

Ouch.

For many years I have made an attempt to figure this out and to this day it makes my head hurt to even think about it. You see, I am not wired to understanding anything other than basic economic principles and, until now, have avoided digging into the weeds to understand the nit and grit of monetary policy. My bad.

Sadly, the time has come to become educated on the reality of money and its first cousin wealth. Like it or not, remaining oblivious to how money affects our ability to survive will result in unilateral wealth reduction and if that happens we will be in a pickle, with no food, no medicine, and no stuff to sustain even a modicum of comfort.

Let me be clear: When I say "wealth", I am not referring to having a net worth of millions or even thousands. That is because wealth comes in many forms, including but not limited to skills, emergency stockpiles, family, and even friends. In addition to money, of course.

Given my avoidance of all things economic, when Ron Brown asked me to critique his new book, *Prepper's Guide to Wealth*, I said bring it on. He warned me in advance that, while it was short, it would likely clarify my understanding of currency and how it is controlled in the modern world.

What he did not tell me is that towards the end of the book there is a call to action that anyone and everyone can embrace should our country descend to the depths of socialism. Think Venezuela and Cuba.

I'm not going to be a spoiler but will share this: if you believe in preparing for your future, no matter what the circumstances, you will be happy you read this book. You will also be a lot smarter.

Just sayin',

Gaye

SIDE NOTE: Gaye's bio is the next-to-last item in the Table of Contents, above.

So Let Us Begin

I wrote this in 2019. Then tucked it away and promptly forgot about it. But today (2021) I found it again. I read it over and thought it worth updating and sharing. Its purpose is to help the reader, presumably a prepper, make sound investment decisions. Twenty years ago it would have been a discussion comparing stocks and bonds to precious metals and real estate. And those are still valid topics. But today we must add negative interest rates, the elimination of cash, and bitcoin to the mix.

Please know that this write-up does not include ways to cheat the system. For example, I've heard of folks accumulating a lot of student debt and then declaring bankruptcy. Whee! Free ride! Please know that Sneaky Pete stuff like that is *not* part of this book.

Although it may be wishful thinking on my part, I'd like to believe that this book presents and compares *investing* strategies and not just *speculative* strategies. In the stock market, puts and calls and short-selling are speculative whereas "buy-and-hold" is an investment. Currency trading (swapping back and forth between Swiss francs and U.S. dollars, for example) is another speculation. But, having said that, I must admit the boundary between "investing" and "speculating" can get pretty fuzzy at times.

Intrinsic Value

Let us wax philosophical for a moment. Money is used both as a medium of exchange and as a store of value. Many different things — both tangible (wampum) and intangible (bitcoin) — can serve as money. All of which makes "money" rather difficult to define.

Aristotle (384 BC - 322 BC) said that "money" should be (1) durable, (2) portable, (3) divisible, (4) consistent, and (5) have intrinsic value.

The first three characteristics are self-explanatory. Number 4, *consistency*, draws attention to the shortcomings of a commodity like grain being used for money. Grain is inconsistent (e.g. heavy if wet and lightweight if dry). But *intrinsic value*? That's where we can really get hung up.

The intrinsic value of a manufacturing company is its future earnings potential. **Repeat:** *The intrinsic value of a manufacturing company is its future earnings potential.* We'll come back to that later.

But how about silver and gold? Do they have intrinsic value?

Silver is used in jewelry and thus has an *ornamental* value. But silver is also an industrial metal. It's the best conductor of electricity known so it's used in printed circuit boards and solar panels. That gives silver a *utilitarian* value. But does that translate into *intrinsic* value? Silver has been used in the past both as coined money and as backing for paper money.

> Silver has the highest electrical conductivity of all metals. In fact, silver defines conductivity — all other metals are rated against it. On a scale of 0 to 100, silver ranks 100 with copper at 97 and gold at 76.
> https://www.lehigh.edu/~amb4/wbi/kwardlow/conductivity.htm

Gold is used in jewelry and thus has *ornamental* value. And the connecting "fingers" on printed circuit boards are plated with gold — albeit with a thickness in the 0.25μ to 5μ (micron) range — to resist corrosion. That's a more *utilitarian* value than a generation ago when gold was used for dental fillings and little else. So does gold have *intrinsic* value? I'll let you answer that one. Like silver, gold has been used in the past both as coined money and as the backing for paper money.

Please note that an item's rarity does not necessarily make it a good money candidate. Nor a good store-of-value candidate. A baseball signed by Babe Ruth is both rare and valuable. As a collectible it makes a fair store of value. A baseball signed by me is far more rare. But far less valuable.

It hurts my head to think so much.

Monetary History — How Did We Get Here?

In 1900, President McKinley signed the Gold Standard Act which made gold the sole basis of U.S. paper dollars. It set the value of gold at $20.67 per ounce and the value of a paper dollar at 25.8 grains of gold.

In 1933, President Roosevelt confiscated gold from U.S. citizens and paid them $20.67 paper dollars per ounce for what they turned in. Once he had everyone's gold in hand, Roosevelt changed the price of gold to $35 per ounce (thereby handing himself a 69% profit). It was illegal for U.S. citizens to own gold (except jewelry). U.S. citizens could own paper dollars "backed" by gold but they could not redeem those dollars for the metal itself. The government reserved unto itself the privilege of owning gold. It would, however, if need be, pay *foreign* claims in physical gold. But U.S. citizens were limited to owning paper dollars, a proxy for gold.

In 1944, near the end of World War II (when it became clear as to which side was winning), delegates from 44 countries met in Bretton Woods, New Hampshire, to design a new world financial system to be put in place after the war.

World Wars I and II were fought on foreign soil, not U.S. soil. The U.S. was shielded by the Atlantic Ocean on one side and the Pacific Ocean on the other. Many countries sent their gold to the U.S. for safekeeping. By the end of World War II, the U.S. held 75% of all the physical gold in the free world.

Prior to World War I, most countries had a gold-backed currency. Their paper money was redeemable in gold. After Bretton Woods, only the U.S. dollar was redeemable in gold. All other currencies were redeemable in U.S. dollars — valued at $35 U.S. paper dollars per ounce.

We immediately began cheating, of course, printing more dollars than we had gold. Twenty years later we discovered the Viet Nam war to be very expensive. The French, who never quite trusted us anyway, began refusing paper dollars and demanding physical gold. Finally, on August 15, 1971, I watched President Nixon on TV declare the U.S. would not pay out any more gold.

Nixon slammed shut the "gold window" and we broke our promise. We defaulted on Bretton Woods. The U.S. dollar was officially delinked or disconnected from gold. Since that time — 1971 — the dollar has been a fiat currency, no longer backed by gold or any other physical commodity. The U.S. dollar today has no *intrinsic* value. It merely "floats" against the other currencies of the world to establish a *relative* value.

"Fiat" is defined as an arbitrary order or decree. "Fiat money" is paper money declared legal tender by decree, not backed by gold or silver or anything else. "I hereby declare this piece of paper to be money," the king pronounces. Why is it money, you ask? "Because I say so!" thunders the king. **That** is fiat money. And it's what we have in the U.S. today (2021).

There have been 700 fiat currencies in the history of the world (or so I've read). And they've all failed. Every. Single. One. Except the U.S. dollar.

Shirley Temple smiles and says, "That's because the dollar is special. It's on a different track." My pessimistic side disagrees, "Be real. There's only one track. Sooner or later the dollar will also fail. It's the nature of the critter. Failure is *inevitable*. The only question is *when?*"

In 1974 it became legal, once again, for U.S. citizens to own gold. And why not? By that time it was just another metal. It no longer had any connection to printed currency.

Then, 35 years later, in 2009, along came bitcoin. Bitcoin can serve as money — albeit electronic money — a blip of light on a computer screen, a magnetic pattern on a spinning disc, a minute static discharge from a capacitor, a radio wave bounced off a satellite. Granted, it's not even paper. At best it's a bookkeeping entry . . . computerized, of course.

Bitcoin is a private endeavor, completely independent of the U.S. dollar and the U.S. government and the banking system and the Federal Reserve System. And, just like the U.S. dollar, bitcoin is not backed by anything and has no intrinsic value. Gee. Sounds like "money" to me.

So, in round numbers, that's where we are today and how we got here.

How Will Negative Rates Impact Me?

Earlier in my life, the business model for banks was that they paid you, the customer, 3% interest on savings and charged you 6% on loans. Not too difficult to understand.

But today we're talking about negative interest rates? Really? *Negative?*

Yes, really. The world has changed.

Today (2021), three countries are listed as having negative interest rates (Japan, Denmark, and Switzerland). But 22 other countries have zero rates so they're catching up fast. You can't stand in the way of progress, eh?
https://tradingeconomics.com/country-list/interest-rate

A negative bank interest rate of 1% per month would mean that on January 1st, say, you have a bank balance of $1000 and, a month later, on February 1st, it will be $990. At the end of one year your balance would be $886.

Today, your $1000 bank balance can be withdrawn and used to purchase 1000 bars of soap or 2000 candles. If you wait twelve months before making the withdrawal, you'll be able to buy 886 bars of soap or 1772 candles.

If you had simply stuffed $1000 cash in your mattress you'd still have $1000 twelve months later. But, fart smeller that you are, you put your $1000 in the bank and lost 11.4% of your purchasing power.

Mattress-stuffing with cash attempts to defeat negative interest rates. But mattress-stuffing with cash requires cash. To prevent mattress stuffing with cash, the banks must eliminate cash. (Or mattresses.) But then again, maybe they don't have to eliminate cash after all. Consider this . . .

The Game Plan Revealed

There's an IMF (International Monetary Fund) statement on the "IMF Blog" dated Feb. 5, 2019 by Ruchir Agarwal and Signe Krogstrup. It reveals, I believe, whence we are headed. https://blogs.imf.org/2019/02/05/cashing-in-how-to-make-negative-interest-rates-work/

> "The proposal is for a central bank to divide the monetary base into two separate local currencies — cash and electronic money (e-money). E-money would be issued only electronically and would pay the policy rate of interest, and cash would have an exchange rate — the conversion rate — against e-money. This conversion rate is key to the proposal. When setting a negative interest rate on e-money, the central bank would let the conversion rate of cash in terms of e-money depreciate at the same rate

as the negative interest rate on e-money. The value of cash would thereby fall in terms of e-money.

"To illustrate, suppose your bank announced a negative 3 percent interest rate on your bank deposit of 100 dollars today. Suppose also that the central bank announced that cash-dollars would now become a separate currency that would depreciate against e-dollars by 3 percent per year. The conversion rate of cash-dollars into e-dollars would hence change from 1 to 0.97 over the year. After a year, there would be 97 e-dollars left in your bank account. If you instead took out 100 cash-dollars today and kept it safe at home for a year, exchanging it into e-money after that year would also yield 97 e-dollars.

"At the same time, shops would start advertising prices in e-money and cash separately, just as shops in some small open economies already advertise prices both in domestic and in bordering foreign currencies. Cash would thereby be losing value both in terms of goods and in terms of e-money, and there would be no benefit to holding cash relative to bank deposits.

"This dual local currency system would allow the central bank to implement as negative an interest rate as necessary for countering a recession, without triggering any large-scale substitutions into cash."

My own take on the situation is . . . *at last! The game plan revealed!* Not pretty. But at least we know what we're facing. You can't address the problem if you can't identify the problem.

Bitcoin shook up the financial world. A more generic term for bitcoin is cryptocurrency. Bitcoin is a brand name just like Colgate is a brand name for (generic) toothpaste. "Bitcoin" was the original cryptocurrency so, in common parlance, it's often used when the generic term "cryptocurrency" would be more accurate.

Proper cryptocurrencies are all based on blockchain — a distributed ledger. For the moment, the important thing to know is that e-money (discussed above) is not the same as cryptocurrency. E-money is not necessarily based on blockchain. It may be computerized and it may look like cryptocurrency but e-money is merely an electronic bookkeeping entry. You might describe e-money as counterfeit crypto.

The Dilemma of a Money System

Greece, suffering many economic woes in recent years, has given birth to several local money schemes. The best known is "TEM" (Alternative Money Unit), created in 2015. You can Google for it.

Ithaca Hours (just up the road from where I live) began in 1991 and was the oldest local currency in the USA (ref. *Hometown Money, 2nd Edition* by Paul Glover, 86 pages, 1995). I say "was" because it's no longer in use. But there are others. "Time Dollars" is one example. "LETS" (Local Exchange Trading System) is another.

Local money systems soon reveal that money has two functions. One is to facilitate trade. It's hard to barter a cow for a haircut. But the second function of money is to store wealth. You can earn (and save) money when you're young and healthy. Then spend it when you're old and feeble.

Unfortunately, the "store wealth" function destroys the "facilitate trade" function. If you hoard (tangible, physical paper) Ithaca Hours it removes them from circulation and the money supply dries up. And then what happens to the Ithaca-Hour money system? Kaput.

U.S. dollars (the official U.S. currency) comprise a large enough pool (of both tangible paper and intangible bank balances) that considerable saving (hoarding) can be tolerated and commerce can continue unhindered. But a threshold does exist beyond which damage is done. Too many savers and not enough spenders means that consumption — i.e. the economy — will be negatively impacted.

Ironically, when we have a recession and people lose their jobs, they get worried and become savers. Their cautionary saving takes additional money out of circulation and makes the recession worse. So the "consumption economy" is at eternal war with the "wealth preservation" side of the world.

What Are Negative Rates Supposed to Accomplish?

Negative rates are intended to discourage you from saving money and encourage you to spend money. Spending stimulates the economy.

That's the plan but it's in conflict with the consumer who's trying to protect himself by saving for the future. "Saving for a rainy day" has been preached as a virtue for as long as I can remember.

Unfortunately "the economy" needs the consumer to spend his money, not hoard it. Else the economy dies.

With a negative 1% per month rate, today's $1000 in the bank will become $886 a year from now. Traditionally, I'd be better off withdrawing my $1000 from the bank today and squirreling it away in my mattress. Then I'd still have $1000 a year later.

From the bankers' point of view, *saving* printed dollars impedes the negative-interest-rate *spending* incentive and must therefore be eliminated. But accepting the bank's rationale requires a reversal of my own thinking. I've been taught lifelong that "thrift" and "saving" are virtuous. Now I'm being told that thrift and saving are selfish; thrift and saving are uncharitable as regards the health of the economy and the greater good.

Side Effects of Negative Rates

At first blush, it seems like eliminating savers will do long-term harm to the economy. Without savers there will be no pool of money to lend entrepreneurs for new business ventures. Then again, because fiat money can be created out of thin air at the stroke of a pen, perhaps savers are superfluous today and we don't need them anymore. Hmm.

But back to the short term. If your paycheck goes direct to the bank and all your bills are paid electronically from that bank balance then it will give your bank total visibility (not to mention control) over your spending. That's a significant side effect of eliminating cash. True, with no cash in the system the authorities can achieve their official goal — creating negative interest rates — but they will also gain visibility to every transaction you make. They'll be able block or stop any transaction they don't like. Picture yourself putting your debit card in the card reader at checkout and having it go tilt. No tobacco for you. No vodka for you. No airline ticket for you. They can stop a diabetic from purchasing chocolate. Naughty, naughty.

They can stop you from withdrawing or transferring funds. They can decide whether to return your deposit to you or not. They might just decide to keep it for themselves — call it "Civil Forfeiture Made Easy."

"Civil forfeiture [used during Prohibition] allows police to seize — and then keep or sell —any property they allege is involved in a crime. Owners need not ever be arrested or convicted of a crime for their cash, cars, or even real estate to be taken away permanently by the government. Forfeiture was originally presented as a way to cripple large-scale criminal enterprises by diverting their resources. But today . . . [many] seizures [are] motivated by profit [the proceeds going to the local police department] rather than crime-fighting."
https://www.aclu.org/issues/criminal-law-reform/reforming-police-practices/asset-forfeiture-abuse

". . . in 2014 alone, federal agents [using civil forfeiture] seized more than $5 billion — an amount greater than what was lost in every single burglary in

America that year." — *Surviving Fedcoin* by Casey Research, 2016

In summary, even if negative rates are themselves a good thing (accomplished by replacing cash with e-money), giving the government total visibility and control over what you spend will produce some very disagreeable side effects.

Black Markets

I've not seen this discussed elsewhere but eliminating ALL cash will not be allowed to happen.

The quickest way to jack up the price of a commodity is to make it illegal. Alcohol during Prohibition (1920-1933) is the classic example.

Black markets materialize to supply the forbidden item. But follow the money. I've always suspected that the folks who make the laws forbidding something are the same folks who profit from the black market that emerges. And black markets operate on good ol' untraceable cash.

Today's black market for drugs requires anonymous cash in the hands of buyers. The black market for drugs would collapse without it. No cash = no black markets.

And drug dealers bribe politicians. No cash = no black markets = no bribe-money. As I said, that ain't gonna happen. The people who make the laws, and the people who bribe the people who make the laws, will move heaven and earth to keep cash in the system.

That's why the IMF proposal discussed at the beginning of this write-up (i.e. cash and e-money being issued together and forced to stay at par) will *succeed*. Because it makes provision for cash. Even though it's a steadily depreciating cash, it's still anonymous. And that will allow black markets to continue. (Man. These central-banker dudes think of everything.)

Please note, however, that all cash is not created equal. The printed U.S. dollars you hoard today will be useless then. Today's printed money will be replaced with a new design. And there will be limits on how much old cash you'll be allowed to exchange for new.

The official intent of the conversion will be to render today's suitcases of $100 bills (be they counterfeit or be they real) worthless. Those are the suitcases currently held outside the USA by drug lords.

When the new currency is issued (and you've waited in line outside the bank for several hours to exchange old-design money for new), if you have *too much* old cash to exchange — i.e. an amount that's suspicious in the eyes of the bank teller serving you — then be prepared for a tacky interview with the bank's security people. (Perhaps you should memorize your lawyer's phone number before you even go to the bank. Call it prepping.)

The Magic of Negative Interest Rates

Following is a (heavily) edited transcript from the *Keiser Report*, March 19, 2019, episode E1359.
https://www.rt.com/shows/keiser-report/454182-debt-economy-negative-rates/

Tweet from Lisa Abramowicz (for discussion purposes): "The pool of negative-yielding debt has risen to a new post-2017 high of $9.2 trillion . . . This is the market value of Bloomberg-Barclays Global Aggregate Negative-Yielding Debt Index."

Stacy Herbert: "This shows that bankers are terrified. To the point they're willing to lose money by lending at a negative rate."

Max Keiser: "Up until recently the idea of a negative interest rate was considered a financial impossibility. It had never been tried before in the history of economics — ever — back to Adam Smith and *The Wealth of Nations* in 1776. There's never, ever been a try, before, of a negative interest rate.

"But like they discovered in the world of physics last week, they've now proven time can go backwards. Right? Up until recently that's been considered an impossibility. But it's the same thing as negative interest rates. Impossible, but yet it's there. It's a fancy way of confiscation.

"Banks are imploding, dying. But instead of allowing them to die as they should have, years ago, they've been supported with cheap interest rates. But they still are not avoiding collapse. So now they must perform wealth confiscation — negative interest rates. Coming to your bank account soon. It's a soft bailout — a soft bail-in, effectively."

Stacy: "We've warned [for a long time] that negative rates are coming. Negative rates were considered impossible because every economic theory — the Austrian school, Keynesianism — was proposed prior to 1971."

Max: "In 1971 there was a bold experiment [when President Nixon abrogated the Bretton Woods agreement and stopped redeeming U.S. dollars for gold]. It tried something never before done — every currency in the world was to be backed by other fiat money. Gold was removed entirely. There was no currency in the world backed by anything. For the first time in history all currencies were backed by each other. It's called 'infinite regress.' All controlled by the Bank of International Settlements and the world's central banks who colluded in a massive conspiracy to pretend the banks aren't collapsing.

"But they are [collapsing]. We have proof of that with the $9.2 trillion [mentioned in the *tweet* at the beginning of this article] and negative interest rates. Every major bank —JP Morgan, Deutsche Bank, BNP — is insolvent by hundreds of billions.

"In 2008, when it was time to sell some of the bonds that were on the books of these banks, as a way to pay off their debts, we discovered the value of those bonds, on the market, was not a hundred cents on the dollar, like the banks were telling us, but actually closer to one or two cents on the dollar. That's how we know they're insolvent. Because there's no market for these bonds. They're unsellable.

"I can claim that I own the Brooklyn Bridge. And I can sell a multi-billion bond against the Brooklyn

Bridge. Well, eventually somebody's gonna come and say, 'Deliver.' And I'll say, 'I can't. I don't have the deed.' Just like the 2008 sub-prime crisis. There were no deeds for the houses that Goldman Sachs packaged as collateral for mortgage obligations and sold into the pension market. They didn't have the deeds. They were just pulling rabbits out of their hat, selling them as 'yielding securities' to pension funds."

My Reaction: Holy schmoly!

How Big Is a Trillion?

The *Keiser Report* (above) mentions the number $9.2 trillion a couple of times. And we hear the term "trillion" quite often these days. But how big is a trillion? It's hard to wrap your head around.

In 1981, President Reagan described a trillion dollars as follows: "If you had a stack of thousand-dollar bills in your hand only 4 inches high, you'd be a millionaire. A trillion dollars would be a stack of thousand-dollar bills 67 miles high." Once more with feeling. *Holy schmoly!*

Granted, Reagan's numbers are rounded. But they're close enough for talking purposes. If you find the 67-mile figure hard to swallow, just do the arithmetic. A dollar bill is .004375 inches thick. Presumably a $1000 bill (if there were such a thing) would be the same. There are 12 inches in a foot and 5,280 feet in a mile. That's all you need to know. Go for it.

Today (2021) the national debt is $29 trillion. That's a stack of $1000 bills nearly 2000 miles high. That's up where the satellites live. Gonna be one helluva crash when one of those satellites bumps that stack of money.

3/28/2019 HEADLINE: *The True Size Of The U.S. National Debt, Including Unfunded Liabilities, Is 222 Trillion Dollars* by Michael Snyder.
http://endoftheamericandream.com/archives/the-true-size-of-the-u-s-national-debt-including-unfunded-liabilities-is-222-trillion-dollars

So how tall is *that*? 14,874 miles? Wow! It's only 6,738 miles New York to Japan. How about grains of sand? 222 trillion grains of sand would weigh over half a million tons.

Sadly, after a while it all becomes gibberish. How much higher can we build the stack before it collapses? *That* is the question.

Gold

Doug Casey is a well-known author and financial advisor. He's also a "gold bug."

"Fedcoin" is Casey's name for what he envisions as a future, government-sponsored equivalent of bitcoin. He's convinced that (1) Fedcoin is a future certainty and that (2) with the advent of Fedcoin, the government will eliminate printed currency. To survive, Casey recommends holding six months' worth of printed currency (for short-term emergency use) in addition to both gold and silver (ref. *Surviving Fedcoin* by Casey Research, 2016).

IMHO we need to modify Casey's conclusion about the elimination of cash. Casey hypothesizes that cash will be eliminated whereas the 2019 IMF recommendation (see above) provides for a continuation of hand-to-hand cash.

Once we get past the cash issue, however, the rest of Casey's ideas appear valid.

Casey says (and I agree) it will take a crisis (real or contrived) to install Fedcoin. And liquid, spendable cash will be essential during the transition period. But after that (in Casey's view), printed currency will become worthless. That's where tangible assets enter the picture. To a gold bug, after all, gold is the only "real" money that exists. All else is smoke and mirrors.

So it makes sense to start our discussion of portfolio holdings with gold. My own point, as you'll no doubt see, is that gold investments entail risks just like anything else. Gold-bug evangelicals tend to skip over that part.

• For example, private gold ownership was illegal in the USA from 1934 to 1974. And it could happen again. You might be forced to surrender your gold at whatever price the government specifies. (Hopefully it will be for more than what you paid.)

• Capital gains tax. If the government ever wants to remove gold from circulation (because it competes with Fedcoin as a form of money, say) they would most likely achieve that goal via a capital gains tax of 95% in preference to criminalizing gold ownership and sending jack-booted storm troopers door-to-door to ransack private homes.

Let's say you buy a gold coin from a dealer for $1000. Two years later, gold doubles in price. You sell the coin back to the dealer. He has a 20% profit margin (that's how he stays in business) so you receive $1800. The government taxes you $760 (95% of your $800 profit). It's all nice and legal but you just risked $1000 to make $40. Plus, due to inflation, the purchasing power of your original $1000 capital diminished over your two-year holding period.

So a capital gains tax could really and truly kill gold's appeal as an investment. Even if you're already stocked up, a future capital gains tax (not yet in existence as I write this) could leave you holding the bag.

• Foreign holdings. Metal detectors make gold smuggling somewhat problematic. And where will you store your gold in a foreign country? Bank safety deposit boxes (if, as a U.S. citizen, you can even get one) will guard against "common thieves" but not against government thieves. And how will you bring your gold home when you need it? And what will it cost you to convert it back to common, spendable currency? It gets very complicated very fast.

If you do wish to hold physical gold in a foreign country, a trusted friend or relative already living in a foreign land (with a secure home safe) would be a decent place to start. *However,* should a Covid-type pandemic result in cross-border travel restrictions, how would you gain access to your gold in your trusted friend's secure safe? Serious question, this.

• Counterfeiting. The specific gravity of gold is 19.32; of tungsten, 19.25. (Lead, incidentally, is 11.34.) Here's a link to a Forbes article from 2012 about gold bars being drilled out and filled with tungsten:
https://www.forbes.com/sites/timworstall/2012/03/26/the-drilled-gold-bars-filled-with-tungsten/#17f82d034e13.
And a Reuter's story on the same topic:
https://www.reuters.com/article/idUS103653650320120325.

Cynics even speculate about the purity of the gold in Fort Knox. The difficulties that countries have in auditing their own gold, much less reclaiming it and taking it home, does nothing to dispel those fears.

"Germany had about 1,200 tons of gold, worth about US$ 50 billion, deposited in the FED in New York. In 2013, when the . . . Bundesbank wanted to withdraw and repatriate all of their foreign stored gold by 2020, the FED said no, they could not deliver. The gold was simply not available." https://journal-neo.org/2019/03/25/la-rinconada-the-devil-s-paradise/

• Physical gold versus paper gold. Gold bugs recommend holding physical gold rather than "paper gold." Mutual funds and ETF's (Exchange Traded Funds) represent, they say, a mere *claim* on gold. Unfortunately, there are more claims on gold than there is metal to support the claims. It should come as no surprise that physical in-hand metal is touted as a safer investment (disregarding burglary risk) than paper gold.

One headline from 2015 (Zerohedge) says: *"There Are Now 293 Ounces of Paper Gold for Every Ounce of Physical"* — https://www.indigopreciousmetals.com/news/comex-leveraged-gold-293-to-1/

Holding physical metal is not always possible, however. Many companies sponsor IRA's (Individual Retirement Accounts) for their employees and make matching contributions. The matching funds are great but, in that circumstance, you don't have much control over how your money is invested. A mutual fund specializing in gold mining stocks might be available to you (though probably

29

not) and provide at least some exposure to gold. Better than nothing, I suppose.

● Leverage. Paper gold (in the form of mining stock) does offer an opportunity for leverage. At the moment (September 2021) gold sells for $1800 an ounce. And let's say your mining company spends $1500 an ounce extracting gold from the ground. Your profit is $300 per ounce or 20% over the extraction cost.

Now say gold's selling price increases from $1800 to $2100 per ounce. The value of your physical one-ounce gold coin increases 17% (2100 ÷ 1800 = 1.17).

But your profit from mining is now $600 per ounce, double what it was yesterday. That's a 100% increase in profit margin — $600 versus $300 — and the price of your mining stock will reflect the higher margin.

This is called "leverage." Note that the higher gain requires holding *paper gold* (mining stock) rather than *real gold* (physical coins).

Paper gold has two downsides. (1) In a downturn, paper gold will decrease in value faster than physical (just like it went up). And (2) in an extreme case your brokerage firm might be unreachable (due to bankruptcy, war, or power outage) meaning your paper gold vanishes into thin air (whereas your physical gold coin remains clenched in your hot little hand).

● Coins versus jewelry. Gold bugs sometimes advocate owning gold jewelry (chains, specifically) rather than gold coins. Jewelry will sidestep a government ban on gold ownership and, with gold *chains*, individual links can be pried loose for small purchases. But riddle me this. Would YOU, up close and personal, accept an envelope of loose gold links as payment for a car you were selling?

Also, with jewelry's high mark-up, you'll forever fight the "buy-retail and sell-wholesale" battle. Even used or "pre-owned" gold jewelry on eBay (after adjusting for purity, etc.) sells at a 40% premium over gold bullion whereas a one-ounce, slabbed, PCGS-graded gold coin (common-date with no numismatic value) sells at 15% over bullion.

> PCGS stands for Professional Coin Grading Service. PCGS grades coins on a numeric scale, 70 being the highest number. After grading, coins are encased in plastic (i.e. slabbed) protecting them from further wear and tear. PCGS guarantees both the grade and the authenticity of a coin.
> (https://www.pcgs.com/guarantee)
> Ditto for NGC, the Numismatic Guaranty Company, a competing service. https://www.ngccoin.com/coin-grading/ngc-guarantee/

• Inflation protection. Some people want to return to a gold standard. Then (as long as mine output matches population growth) the money supply cannot be inflated. Or so they believe. It's an article of faith. In their view, gold is an immutable, permanent standard.

Bill Bonner is another well-known financial adviser. (And a remarkable analyst of current events, may I add. I read him daily.) And he's another gold bug.

Bonner says that if 5 ounces of gold can buy the DOW, then you should buy stocks. But when it takes 15 ounces of gold to buy the DOW, then you should sell stock and buy gold. Over the past 100 years, using that simple strategy, $100 dollars would have become $43.3 million (13.9% annually). A buy-and-hold stock strategy would only have returned $17.7 million (12.8% annually).

But should you stake your future retirement on Bonner's strategy? For one thing, there were 40 years plunk in the middle of that hundred-year period where it was not even legal for an American to own gold. So in practice Bonner's strategy is, or was, a *non sequitur*.

Along the same lines, although never mentioned in polite company, the New York Stock Exchange was actually closed for five months at the beginning of World War I. Bonner's hundred-year timeframe sidesteps that episode.

Gold bugs notwithstanding, in the past, the gold-money supply did indeed surge and cause inflation; gold lost purchasing power. It happened due to **conquest** (plundered Inca gold being shipped to Europe in high volume), **discovery** (in California, Australia, Alaska), and **technology**. In 1877, a commercially viable cyanide process was introduced for extracting gold from low-grade ore. Over 90% of all the gold ever recovered by man has come out of the ground since then.

• Alchemy. Speaking of technology, we live in the atomic age. Historically, "alchemy" has a bad name. But today, it's been demonstrated that *nuclear transmutation* can indeed turn lead into gold.
https://en.wikipedia.org/wiki/Nuclear_transmutation

Granted, the expense of doing so far exceeds any gain. But it can be done. If it ever becomes economically viable there will be great wailing and gnashing of teeth amongst the True Believers. Do you remember when diamonds could not be manufactured by human beings? I do.

• In conclusion, a friend mine — a successful investor — reviewed the manuscript of this book before publication and wrote me: "I find the discussion of gold rather negative. It confuses me. What am I supposed to *do*?"

Actually, there's a reason for me not telling you, the reader, what to do or what action to take.

As a human being, as soon as I recommend something — as regards gold or the stock market or cryptocurrency — I shoulder the role of defending that recommendation. Even if it turns out to be wrong. As a human being I'll defend and rationalize that recommendation to the ends of the earth. That's what people do. You see it all the time. And I'd like to avoid that trap.

Instead, I want YOU to decide what's best for you. I don't have an agenda. I'm not a gold bug or a crypto evangelist. My job is to provide the pros and cons of various investment choices. I've tried to include info that's unique; that you won't see anywhere else; explained with a clarity you won't find elsewhere. But then *you*, the reader — young or old, sick or healthy, rich or poor, male or female — must decide what looks best for you. My answer (about what's best for me) might not be your answer. Fair enough?

Broadening Our Understanding

Hopefully, this write-up will enhance our understanding of various issues related to wealth preservation. But there's more to it than individual portfolio components (gold or real estate or cryptocurrency). Equally important is the *environment* surrounding our investments. Do we live in wartime or peace? Feast or famine? Dictatorship or democracy?

As I write this today (in the USA, in the year 2021) the baby-boom phenomenon that began after World War II will soon come to an end. The boomers are gonna die. And that will have a big impact on the stock market.

Point is, the *environment* in which the stock market operates is just as important to our wellbeing as the selection of individual stocks within the market.

Baby Boomers & Going Short

I foresee a GBDO (Great Boomer Die-Off) that will be very bad news for the stock market.

VE Day (Victory in Europe) was May 8, 1945. VJ Day (Victory in Japan) was August 6th and/or 9th of 1945. In the months following, thousands upon thousands of GI's came home to the USA. In 1946 there was a veritable boom of babies. "How did this happen?" was the question on every tongue.

Answer. The usual way.

The abnormally high birth rate continued through 1959. (Please note that the U.S. Census Bureau defines baby boomers as those persons born between 1946 and 1964. For purposes of this analysis, based on birthrate, 1959 is the more appropriate endpoint.)

The baby-boom phenomenon was real. I was born in 1940, just one step ahead of the boomers. I sat in my elementary school classroom, looking out the window at the new school being built for the boomers. At university I jumped over ditches and circled bulldozers constructing the new libraries and the new gymnasiums being built for the boomers.

In the 1980's, thinking about future retirement, I went out of my way in Florida to visit Marcos Island, as far south as you could drive on the Gulf side. From my reading, it sounded relatively unspoiled, well off the beaten track. I drove over the bridge and, to my dismay, saw the rotating cranes. The high-rise condos, still under construction, stretched to the horizon. I circled the island. Every square inch was scheduled for paving. They were getting ready for the boomers. The boomers who would, in a few short years, retire.

So what's next?

Death.

For sure the boomers will someday die. According to the Social Security Administration, a man born in 1945 will, if he reaches 65 years old, have a remaining life expectancy of 12.6 years.

The baby boom started in 1946. So in 2024 (only three years from now) all the male boomers born in 1946 will, on average, be dead. That will be the kick-off. A year later, in 2025, all the male boomers born in 1947 will be dead. A year after that . . .

The boomer birth-period, from 1946 to 1959, is 13 years. Adding 13 years to the 2024 start point (plus two additional years for female life expectancy) and we can estimate a GBDO end point of 2039. I'll still be around, barely, if I live to be a hundred.

So what can we expect over the 15-year Great Boomer Die-Off? Well, boomers, like everybody else, have accumulated wealth all their lives. But in the last couple of years, just before they die, they'll liquidate it . . . and give it to the doctors and the hospitals and the pharmacies . . . to stay alive a few more years, a few more months, a few more days.

Every asset class will hit the auction block. Stocks, bonds, real estate, precious metals, art, tangible assets, everything. It will all nosedive. The boomers, now old and sick, will be selling. The market will be flooded. Asset values will go down.

It does seem rather predictable. Just like the boomers went to school and graduated and went to work and got married and had babies and got divorces and retired (1946 + 65 years = 2011). All predictable. Today Marcos Island is booming. But between 2024 and 2039 the boomers will die. There'll be a lot of empty condos on Marcos Island.

IMHO, a couple of things are sure to happen: (1) the boomers will sell off their financial assets to pay medical costs and avoid dying (2) the stock market will go down as a result. There will be more sellers than buyers. No amount of flap-jaw from the politicians and interest-rate jiggling by the Federal Reserve will change that.

And how do you make money in a declining market?

Answer. By going short.

It's a wager — you can't really call it an "investment" — that the market will go down and not up. But it is possible to make money in a declining market. And "short selling" is how it's done.

DYODD is a stock-market acronym meaning Do Your Own Due Diligence. And when it comes to short selling, DYODD. Big-time.

Googling for "short selling how to" will generate an impressive list of web pages and videos on the topic. I do believe it's something we all need to learn before the baby boomers die. But I must confess that I, personally, have experimented with short selling and have lost money more often than not. So DYODD! The potential is certainly there but you'll probably find it an expensive learning process. I know I have.

• **CAUTION**. In simple terms, "short-selling" is when you (1) borrow shares of a company from your broker, (2) sell those shares at today's price, and (3) buy back those shares in the future (at a lower price) to repay the loan from your broker.

Note that if you simply *buy* some stock (i.e. go long on the stock), the most you can *lose* is the amount you invested. If the stock's price goes to zero then, yes, your dollar investment is lost. On the other hand (with "going long") your *profit* can go to infinity. In 2011 you could have gone long and purchased one bitcoin — granted it's not a stock but the principle is the same — for 30¢. Eleven years later (Nov. 8, 2021) one bitcoin was over $68,000.

If you *go short* on a security, the consequences are reversed. It's your *loss* that can go to infinity (and bankrupt you in the process). "An investor who had a short position of 100 shares in GameStop as of Dec. 31, 2020, would be faced with a loss of . . . $30,616 if the short position was still open [one month later] on Jan. 29, 2021. Because the stock soared from $18.84 to $325.00 over this one-month period, the investor's return would be *minus* 1,625%." (That's for one month. Let's not annualize that figure, OK?) https://www.investopedia.com/ask/answers/how-does-one-make-money-short-selling/

Profit-wise, if the short-seller (1) borrows a security and (2) sells it and (3) the security value drops to zero . . . then (4) the borrower does not have to repay the lender. So the short-seller makes a profit equal to the amount he borrowed. But that's the upper limit; the best the short-seller can do.

Or so they say. But consider "bear-market" *mutual funds* — funds that go up when securities go down. RYAIX is one such fund. You could have purchased RYAIX on March 24, 2000 for $328. And sold it on September 27, 2002 (30 months later) for $985. You'd have tripled your money. (The DOW lost 32% over that same period.)

"Bear-market funds" are also called "reverse index funds" and "inverse index funds."

All you have to do is determine *when* the stock market is going to crash. And then buy into your bear-market fund a day or two before the crash occurs. What's so hard about that?

Land

In the interest of staving off boredom, I've decided to bounce back and forth, within in this write-up, between our investing *environment* (baby boomers, what happened in Cyprus, etc.) and *portfolio components* (gold, bitcoin, and the like). So let's now switch our discussion away from our "investing environment" and over to the merits of *land* as a portfolio holding.

There's a difference between "land" and "real estate." Real estate includes not just land but any houses or buildings that are on the land. For me, real estate (with buildings) is not a great portfolio holding because buildings require constant, ongoing maintenance. "Land" is more of a passive holding like a bank account or rare coin; upkeep is minimal.

Investment-wise, there are three kinds of land we should consider: farmland, forest land, and campsites with water frontage. There's always a market for accessible, fertile, tillable farmland. Always. And forest land, in addition to future resale value, offers firewood and/or lumber as potential income. And with campsites, well . . . they're not making any more lakes or rivers or water frontage. The supply of campsites with water frontage is not only finite, it's shrinking.

Some people tout land as the ultimate form of wealth. Granted, it is real wealth and underlies most everything else. But it's not perfect. Nothing is. We just need to understand the risks.

If you had to flee Germany in World War II and leave your land behind, establishing ownership in later years was problematic. I've known a few people over the years who struggled to do just that. And if it was East Germany and your land was confiscated by the communist government, then good luck.

In Japan after World War II, Japanese farmland was confiscated by the Americans (i.e. the American-run government) from the wealthy class of Japanese and redistributed to the peasantry.

Fair? Maybe or maybe not. But "fairness" is not the issue. The issue here is keeping your portfolio above the waterline. *Your* portfolio.

And next we have — oh me, oh my — Greece . . .

"Greeks had always seen land as a haven. Home ownership [the percent of people owning rather than renting] . . . is well above the European Union average . . . Old-timers used to urge younger Greeks to buy property to avoid losing savings as they did in frequent currency devaluations — or in the monster inflation during the Axis occupation in World War II. Parents felt duty-bound to help their children acquire homes or leave them property as *the only possible hedge* [emphasis added] against hardship . . . [But] 'We have entered a new era,' said Poppy Kakaidi, a lawyer . . . She has clients who have turned down inheritances . . . In

Athens, the Asylon Aniaton, a hospice, used to fund itself by renting or selling property. Now it's unable to sell anything, and of its 887 properties, 396 are without tenants. In 2015, its revenue came to 2.17 million euros while it had to pay taxes of 1.83 million euros (of which 908,839 euros were property taxes). What was left went toward caring for 180 patients. Property turning toxic . . . which along with tourism could be a pillar of recovery, is not helping . . . It is inconceivable that after six years of crisis such problems would not have been solved." [This was in a 2016 New York Times article.] http://www.nytimes.com/2016/11/02/opinion/in-greece-property-is-debt.html

Turkey, a Muslim country, is right next door to Greece. "On November 11, 1942 . . . the government of the Republican People's Party (CHP), led by the then-prime minister Şükrü Saracoğlu, enacted the Wealth Tax Law. 'The way in which the law was applied was scandalous . . . Converts paid about twice as much as Muslims, while non-Muslims ended up paying up to ten times as much. In addition, non-Muslims were required to pay their taxes in cash within 15 days; as a result, they had to sell their businesses or property to Muslim businessmen at low prices to cover the bill . . .' Those who could not pay the taxes were sent to labor camps, deported, or their properties were seized." https://greekcitytimes.com/2019/11/29/wealth-tax-law-non-muslims-eliminated-economy/

Point is, land is not the end-all and be-all of wealth preservation. Risks do exist. Neighborhoods deteriorate; upscale neighborhoods become slums. Lake frontage goes down in value if the lake becomes polluted. Zoning can change. Industry can move in. Or out (taking jobs with it). Etcetera.

BTW, in some places (e.g. Canada, Belize) a U.S. citizen can own land in his own name. In other places (e.g. Mexico, Philippines) he cannot. He can buy land but the deed must be held in the name of a local citizen (typically the buyer's lawyer).

REITs — Real Estate Investment Trusts — are beyond the scope of this discussion but you should be aware of their existence. REITs are basically mutual funds that invest in real estate. And there are all kinds of REITs. Some specialize in rental properties; others in industrial property. On the plus side, REITs provide access to the profit potential of real estate; they're a way to get a piece of the action. But — in the final analysis — REITs are to land as "paper gold" is to physical gold.

Now here's a question. Looking at your home as an investment and not just living quarters, should you pay off the mortgage? Or should you keep the mortgage and invest the funds — in the stock market, say — that you'd otherwise devote to paying down the mortgage?

Personally, I'd pay it off. Just as I actually did when I retired. I cashed in a 401K and paid off the house. I sleep better knowing that my housing — for the rest of my life — is paid for.

My stockbroker at the time thought I was doing the wrong thing. Plus I have a wealthy friend who advises his children to do exactly the opposite of what I did. Keep the mortgage, he says. It has the lowest interest rate you'll get. Use extra funds to invest in the stock market, not to pay off the mortgage. You'll be further ahead.

I've noodled on that for a bit. It seems to me that, if your primary goal is to *make* money, and if you, psychologically, can handle debt without agonizing over it, then my friend and my broker are correct.

But the thrust of this write-up is wealth *preservation*. If your chief objective is to avoid loss and protect what you already have, then pay off the mortgage.

Remember Sly & the Family Stone? "Different strokes for different folks."

What Happened in Cyprus?

OK, back to the investing "environment" we live in. After the fall of the Berlin Wall in 1989, many businesses from the former Soviet Union moved to Cyprus (an island in the Mediterranean Sea, if you didn't already know). Cyprus offered low corporate taxes, a legal system based on British law, and strict bank-secrecy rules.

In 2012, Cyprus faced a banking crisis. The cause was (as usual) the greed of bankers making risky loans in hopes of high returns. Came the day when both Germany and Russia balked at further bailouts; they stopped throwing good money after bad.

The European Central Bank and the International Monetary Fund told Cyprus the only way it would get the money it needed to stay afloat was to seize deposits at the two largest banks and convert the funds into equity.

So a new word entered our language: "bail-ins" (as opposed to "bailouts"). In 2013, deposits of Cyprus' bank customers were seized and converted into shares of the bank's common stock. Depositors (whether they liked it or not) became shareholders and/or owners of the bank. The deposits had previously been liabilities of the bank (with FDIC-like guarantees). But common stock is, to the bank, neither an asset nor a liability. It is equity.

Note that (in the USA) the FDIC does not guarantee equity. The FDIC only guarantees liabilities in the form of deposits. So a bail-in gets the FDIC sponsor or guarantor off the hook. Slick, yes?

> The *original* Bank of Cyprus announcement was for a 6.75% confiscation of accounts under €100,000 and 9.9% for larger accounts. The final deal was that depositors with over €100,000 would lose 40% while smaller depositors lost nothing.

> I've always suspected the European equivalent of the FDIC came into play. In the European version of FDIC, bank deposits under €100,000 were guaranteed. The original 6.75% confiscation scheme would have violated that guarantee.

You could, of course, take your bank equity shares down to your stockbroker and sell them on the open market for whatever you could get.

As *Forbes* magazine put it in 2013, "A new strategy has been unveiled around the world, with the first test run in Cyprus. Despite early denials, the 'bail-in' strategy for insolvent banks has already become official policy throughout Europe and internationally as well." — https://www.forbes.com/sites/nathanlewis/2013/05/03/the-cyprus-bank-bail-in-is-another-crony-bankster-scam/#2b2725812685

Question. Did the European Central Bank and the IMF and the Cyprus banks get away with this? Answer. Yes. From a legal-challenge point of view, they carried it off without a hitch.

Question. Was the Cyprus bail-in just a dry run to see what they could get away with? Answer. Probably. Cyprus was followed by additional bail-ins in Greece. In my heart of hearts, I expect that, sooner or later, we'll see bail-ins in the United States.

Just to get an idea of the magnitude of what happened, CSE (Cyprus Stock Exchange General Index) tracks the composite performance of all companies listed on the Cyprus Stock Exchange. CSE reached an all-time high of 5518 in October 2007. From there it began a steady long-term decline and today (September 29, 2021) closed at 67, a loss of 98.8%. One hundred dollars invested in 2007 would be $1.20 today (14 years later).

But Wait! There's More . . .

Traditionally, *depositors* are the most senior creditors of a bank. However, "under both the Dodd Frank Act and the 2005 Bankruptcy Act, *derivative claims* have super-priority over all other claims . . ." from *A Crisis Worse than ISIS? Bail-Ins Begin* by Ellen Brown, 2016.
https://www.resilience.org/stories/2016-01-12/a-crisis-worse-than-isis-bail-ins-begin/

Another source says, "Which brings us to the passage of the 2015 federal budget bill, wherein lawmakers repealed a key part of the Dodd-Frank financial reform law, which protected depositors' savings . . .

"In a nutshell, the [2015] budget provision would allow banks to use the savings accounts of Americans to speculate in the markets on behalf of hedge funds, companies, and the rich. Specifically, the banks would use customer savings to help clients make bets on derivatives, the technical financial instruments that were at the center of the [2008] financial crisis."

This comes from an article entitled *Surprise, Surprise! Did You Know That You Don't Own Your Bank Deposits Anymore?* by Susan Duclos, 2015.
http://allnewspipeline.com/Surprise_Surprise_Did_You_Know.php

According to the dictionary, derivatives are: "An arrangement or instrument (such as a future, option, or warrant) whose value *derives from* and is dependent on the value of an underlying asset."

Sounds fancy. But many times a "derivative" is little more than a side bet. I bet $100 that the Yankees win the World Series. And you bet the Dodgers win. The value of our bet is based on — *derives from* — the World Series. The value of our bet is not derived from the price of gold. Or the stock price of IBM. Or the Kentucky Derby. But it could be. Wanna bet?

The long and short of it is this. Today, when you deposit your money in a bank, it becomes the bank's money. It is no longer your money. And if the bank makes a bad bet and loses your money then it's gone forever.

Ah! But there's the FDIC (Federal Deposit Insurance Corporation). They have $41 billion in reserve just to guarantee bank deposits, no?

Well, they did in 2019. As of September 2019 they had $41 billion in reserve to cover $6 trillion in deposits. So every $146 in deposits was guaranteed by one U.S. dollar in reserves.

But in 2020 I read that FDIC reserves were down from $41 billion to $13 billion. If that is true, every dollar in reserve guarantees $462 in deposits. https://askinglot.com/how-much-does-fdic-have-in-reserves

I haven't been able to locate anything more recent than that. Looks like they don't wanna talk about it.

$10,000 Gold

We're discussing several new economic developments in this write-up. New developments related to wealth preservation. One is negative interest rates. Another is bitcoin. Related is the total elimination of cash. Another is e-money and cash with a Fed-specified conversion rate.

One more idea floating around the internet is that gold might be revalued. Investment guru Jim Rickards says that gold will be revalued to $10,000 per ounce. He arrives at that figure by using (1) M1 as a measure of money supply for the world's major economies, (2) 40% gold backing of the money supply, and (3) dividing that number by the official 35,000 tons of gold in the world. https://goldsurvivalguide.co.nz/does-gold-revaluation-to-us10000-with-all-major-countries-make-sense/

You can, of course, use different measures of the money supply and different percentage backing numbers and come up with different answers — ranging from $5,000 to $50,000 an ounce. As Rickards points out, revaluing gold

47

in terms of dollars has actually been done before (though not on this order of magnitude). In 1933 Roosevelt bumped up the price of gold from $20.67 to $35.00 (a 69% increase).

The problem, as I see it, with Rickards' idea being implemented is that dollars are no longer connected to gold. That's why U.S. citizens are allowed to own gold. It's just another metal.

But, for the sake of argument, let's say that the dollar *is* pegged to gold and that Rickards' concern is legitimate. What would the impact be? What is it that you'd need to prep for?

Answer: [1] The dollar would be devalued. [2] The debtor (the U.S. government) could then pay off creditors with devalued currency. Major bond holders (China) would be stiffed, cheated. [3] The purchasing power of the dollars in your pocket would go down; inflation (in dollar terms) would go through the roof. [4] Gold, on the other hand, would zoom in purchasing power. Today, with gold at $1800 per ounce, a $36,000 car costs 20 ounces of gold. Then, with gold at $10,000, the same car would cost less than 4 Krugerrands. My cynical side says that gold ownership would again be made illegal before that was allowed to happen.

Bonds

I must admit that I'm not in love with bonds as an investment. When interest rates go down, bond prices go up. When interest rates go up, bond prices go down. It's a mechanical relationship, built into the nature of the critter.

And where are interest rates right now? Low. Very low. I have a bank account on which I earned one penny of interest last quarter. Meaning bond prices are high. Very high.

At some point, interest rates will go up. And bond prices will go down. And, if I own bonds, I will lose money. Nope. Ain't gonna happen. There are better places to invest.

Silver

I'm gonna walk backwards into this one (rather than plunging in headfirst).

The term *prepping* is an abbreviation of the word *preparing*. But what are we preparing *for?*

The non-prepper says: "Prepare for what? War? Stock market crash? Pandemic? Power grid failure? The Yellowstone volcano? Meltdown of the Indian Point nuclear plant? An eruption of La Palma in the Canary Islands with a tsunami that wipes out the U.S. East Coast? What?"

And the prepper says: "Why don't people try and shield themselves and their loved ones against possible emergencies and disasters? Aren't the risks obvious?"

Personally, I've come to believe that the issue is one of "normalcy bias" or "lineal thinking." Here are three different ways of saying much the same thing:

Wikipedia: "Normalcy bias . . . [is] the assumption . . . that since a disaster never has occurred then it never will occur."

Robert A. Heinlein: "Logic is a way of saying that anything which didn't happen yesterday won't happen tomorrow."

The Great Reckoning by Davidson and Rees-Mogg: "Lineal thinking [can be defined as follows]: Most of the time, most people expect current conditions to continue for the indefinite future . . . This is why cities are built on floodplains and fault lines . . . The existence of nonlinear relationships remains genuinely invisible to most people."

Time for a story.

I worked my entire career as an engineer. Was often called upon to solve production problems. Department XYZ is falling behind . . . or its inventory is screwed up . . . or it has poor quality . . . or a bad safety record . . . or too much downtime . . .

For me, finding the solution was always the easy part. *Selling* the solution was a different kettle of fish. *Selling* was never one of my strong suits.

I retired in 2005. For the last fifteen years of my working life I was in the printed circuit board industry. We used a lot of solder, a tin/lead compound. But lead is not good for you.

A couple of years before I retired, the European Union issued the Restriction of Hazardous Substances Directive

(RoHS). It proclaimed that, effective July 2006, lead-based solder could not be used in consumer goods sold in the EU. Not in goods made in the EU. Not in goods made elsewhere and shipped into the EU. Read my lips. No. More. Lead.

Every cell phone, every TV, every computer has printed circuit boards. And every circuit board contains lead-based solder. What could be substituted? Compounds containing silver, as it turned out.

Of the 70 or 80 possible lead-solder substitutes, 90% of them contained silver. Of the five most likely candidates, *all* contained silver. The economy of the European Union, in total, is slightly larger than the economy of the United States. That's a lot of circuit boards. That's a lot of silver. What do you suppose will happen to the demand for silver, to the price of silver?

And this is not something that just *might* happen. This is something that *will* happen. It's the law. Done deal. Baked in the cake.

Using this "insider information" I went to a local coin dealer and bought some physical silver bars. With shipping they cost me $5.15 an ounce. Silver had held steady at five or six bucks an ounce for all of the previous 15 years.

It was so obvious. But I could not interest any of my coworkers in silver. Not one. And they were in the industry, privy to the same information I had. They looked at me strangely; deer in the headlights. I assumed it was due to my proven track record of superior salesmanship. I quit trying.

By July 2006 (when the EU directive went into effect) I was retired and silver had *doubled* in price; it was $11 an ounce. Another year went by and, in 2007, silver was $15, *triple* what I paid. In 2008 it was $20, *quadruple* what I paid. I made money on that one.

Later on, one of my (ex)coworkers said to me, "Boy, you were lucky with that silver thing."

Say what? My friend, do you have any idea how hard I tried to convince *you* to buy some silver?

In retrospect, I think it was normalcy bias on my coworkers' part moreso than my lack of salesmanship. "The existence of nonlinear relationships remains genuinely invisible to most people."

Now here's a scary thought. Who's to say that the President of Harvard or the CEO of ExxonMobil are any more immune to normalcy bias than the greeter over at Walmart or the engineers I hung out with in the lunchroom (back when I was pushing silver)? Were I a bettin' man, I would wager that the blind spot of lineal thinking is no respecter of college degrees or Stanford-Binet IQ scores or leadership ability.

Leaders in particular seem to have more than their fair share of normalcy bias; it goes with the territory. These are the folks who point their index finger skywards and exhort us to go to the moon or build a Great Wall or go to war.

Normalcy bias explains why nuclear plants (and not just cities) are built on floodplains and fault lines.

If you "get it" you're one of the few. The downside is, as you've no doubt discovered, it's lonely out there.

Back to silver. It is estimated that, above ground, ten ounces of silver exist for every one ounce of gold. You can interpret that as indicating a "natural" price for silver as one-tenth the price of gold. So if gold is $1800 (as it is in 2021) then silver should be $180. But silver is only $22. Somewhat under-valued perhaps?

In the scarcity department, the biggest use for silver (for over a hundred years; until the advent of digital photography) was in photographic film. And used film, both photographic and X-ray, ended up in the city dump. The silver concentration was too low to make reclamation economically viable. So for a hundred years we mined silver, used it, and scrapped it . . . making what remained in inventory a bit scarcer than it would have otherwise been.

So here's my pitch. Silver is the best electrical conductor known. That's why it's in circuit boards and solar panels. As an industrial metal it has utilitarian value and not just ornamental value. It's volatile; it goes up in price and down in price. And that's a good thing. That's how you make money. Buy low and sell high.

So-called "junk silver" coins with no numismatic value (minted 1964 and earlier) are widely available (on eBay as well as at local rare coin shops) and are instantly recognizable. Their purity and silver content is a matter of public record.

And, if you ever need to barter with your junk silver coins or use them in trade, the divisibility problem (due to dimes, quarters, and halves) is mostly resolved. You don't have to buy or sell 100 oz. at a time in the form of a bullion bar.

What's not to like?

India . . . and Cash

On November 8, 2016 (eight days before Donald Trump was elected President), Indian Prime Minister Narendra Modi summoned his ministers to a cabinet meeting.

Modi had his ministers leave their cellphones outside the room, then told them his plan. The ministers were not allowed to leave the room (and tip anybody off) before the plan was announced publically.

Modi then made an unscheduled appearance on primetime television and announced that all old-issue 500-rupee and 1000-rupee notes, the functional equivalent of America's $20 and $100 bills, would no longer be legal tender after midnight, four hours hence.

That represented 86% of all of India's printed cash. Smaller denomination notes (100-rupees and less) would continue to circulate. The 500-rupee and 1000-rupee notes would be replaced with new-design 500-rupee and new-design 2000-rupee notes. The goal was to combat tax evasion and black markets supported by "black money" held outside the official economic system

Modi's plan inflicted a lot of suffering on his country but accomplished little. After two years, one way or another, 99.3% of the old 500-rupee and 1000-rupee notes had been turned in and exchanged.

The point is this. At the stroke of a pen, what had been legal tender was no longer legal tender. Modi's actions were challenged in court but the courts supported Modi. And this should serve as a warning to us all. What you *believe* you have in your pocket as money ain't necessarily so. Your savings, the results of your hard work, your *money* . . . could all disappear . . . legally . . . permanently . . . in the blink of an eye . . . on the whim of a politician.

From the beginning there were exceptions to Modi's ban — 500-rupee and 1000-rupee notes could still be used in hospitals, gas stations, drug stores, and train stations, for example.

For individual Indians, credit cards were not an option. 97% of all transactions in India are cash transactions. There were only 25 million credit cards in India — one card for every 53 people. That's one card per busload of people. In the U.S. there are 364 million cards for 324 million people.

By November 9, one day after Modi made his announcement, a black market sprang up for the banned denominations. You could buy a demonetized 1000-rupee note for 700 rupees in smaller, still-legal denominations. You had to do this on the street, of course, the banks were all closed.

But why would anybody buy the banned currency at any price? Why? Because if you could "prove" you were a hospital, gas station, drug store, or train station, you could deposit the banned cash in your bank account at full face value.

As a result, hospitals refused payment in the still-useable-at-hospital 500/1000 rupee notes. Instead, they demanded payment in 100-rupee (and smaller) notes. THEN the hospitals went on the street (the black market) with hundred-rupee notes in hand and purchased thousand-rupee notes — for 700 rupees. Which they, as a hospital, could deposit in their bank account at face value . . . generating a 43% profit $(1000 \div 700 = 1.43)$.

I was amazed that they got away with it. I have a stockbroker friend who hails from India and who assures me that Indian notes are, by law, "legal tender and nobody can refuse them." But the hospitals did. And got away with it.

Lesson learned. This is how Indians fight corruption.

The government did not have enough replacement bills to carry out the exchange. (And it might take a year to get enough.) Further, the new bills were smaller than the old bills and would not feed properly through the machines intended to dispense them. (And it might take two months to retrofit the machines.) But, if cash was not available for the exchange, you could deposit the money in your bank account . . . as long as it was ahead of the deadline . . . and, BTW, there would be restrictions on how much you could withdraw each week.

The only problem with depositing the old notes was that half the population did not have a bank account. And, of the people who did not have a bank account, half of them lacked the proper identification to get a bank account. One more time, what could possibly go wrong?

Ask the 150 people who died waiting in line at banks and ATM's around the country. Died as in dead. Expired. Deceased. Perished. Croaked.

Unbelievable as it may sound, if someone wanted to convert old currency to new currency, any amount greater than 250,000 rupees ($3,650), would require that person, by law, to explain how they came to have so much cash. And if they couldn't prove they'd paid tax on that cash, they'd be fined 200% percent of the tax owed.

People were clever (as people generally are) at getting around the rules. Some folks used "old cash" to pay a hospital in advance for upcoming medical procedures. Others booked future train travel using old cash and later cancelled. After paying the cancellation charges they got the balance of their refund in new cash.

There were hidden motives behind Modi's currency exchange. The ultimate goal was, and remains, to eliminate printed money, paper folding money. The purpose of eliminating cash is to facilitate negative interest rates. India was a dry run, a test case, to see what worked, what didn't, and how much the government could get away with.

F. William Engdahl is a journalist and political analyst *par excellence*. On January 21, 2017, he wrote:

> "The Modi cash-less India operation is a project of the US National Security Council, US State Department, and Office of the President, administered through its US Agency for International Development (USAID) . . .

"The USAID 'Project Catalyst' in partnership with the Indian Finance Ministry was done, according to the USAID press statement, with . . . [an] organization called CashlessCatalyst.org [whose members include] . . . the Bill & Melinda Gates Foundation, VISA, MasterCard, Omidyar Network [of eBay billionaire founder Pierre Omidyar], the World Economic Forum, etc.

"India . . . implementing [this] . . . agenda is clearly serving as a guinea pig in a mass social experiment about how to push the cash war in other countries."

We probably all agree it's prudent to have a stash of cash on hand for emergencies. But one lesson from India stands out. The cash stash should be in small-denomination bills that won't be confiscated — $10 bills and smaller. If any single U.S. denomination is impounded it will be the $100 bill. With $50's close behind. And $20's probable.

Larry Summers (former Treasury Secretary and advisor to President Obama) called for eliminating the $100 bill — which, alone, represents 76% of all printed U.S. cash.

Peter Sands, a senior fellow at Harvard's Mossavar-Rahmani Center for Business and Government, wants to eliminate the printed U.S. $100 bill as well as all high-denomination currencies in all countries.

Ken Rogoff (the Thomas D. Cabot Professor of Public Policy and Professor of Economics at Harvard and former Chief Economist at the IMF) says the U.S. should get rid of the $20 bill and the $50 bill as well as the $100 bill — 97% of all printed U.S. cash.

At the January 2017 World Economic Forum in Davos, Switzerland, Joseph Stiglitz (Nobel Laureate economist), said that the U.S. should rid itself of physical cash. By that "he means . . . not only get rid of $100 bills but . . . ALL paper currency — 50s, 20s, 10s, 5s, and even 1s." https://www.sovereignman.com/trends/nobel-prize-winner-says-us-should-get-rid-of-currency-20690/

Ah, but that won't happen! No cash at all translates into no black markets and no anonymous bribes. Nope. That will never be allowed to happen.

• *Tip.* If you've saved some rainy-day cash but it's in large bills, and you now want to convert it to smaller bills without drawing attention to yourself, consider a gambling casino. Take some $50 bills to the cashier's window and ask, "Can I get this in tens?"

"Sure. No problem." (Many people, you see, are reluctant to put a $50 bill in a slot machine. But they'll feed in $10 bills, one after another, all night long. The casinos know this.)

But there's a new wrinkle. Today (2021), casinos have "bill breaking machines" (that's what they're called if you Google for them) scattered about the premises. If you have a receipt from a slot machine — be it some winnings or some change left from your original "investment" that you haven't lost yet — you can cash that receipt at a machine instead of standing in line at the teller's window.

Plus, in addition to cashing out receipts, you can break a big bill — a $100 bill or a $50 or even a $20 — into smaller bills at the same machine. You'll get four $5 bills for a $20. And the machine never asks "why" you are doing this. Sweet.

#Notebandi Frontlines: Onion Rates Halve, Farmers Have No Cash, Can't Go Cashless
by Swagata Yadavar reporting in
IndiaSpend, December 16, 2016

https://archive.indiaspend.com/cover-story/notebandi-frontlines-onion-rates-halve-farmers-have-no-cash-cant-go-cashless-50473

"Prime Minister Narendra Modi would be happy with 26-year-old Deepak Patil, a 26-year-old onion farmer . . . about 300 km north of Mumbai [Bombay] . . . he has a bank account, a cell phone, and receives payment for his onion produce in cheque.

"But Patil . . . is not happy with [Modi's] . . . [rupee] demonetisation, or *notebandi* as it is colloquially called.

". . . the government pushed for cashless transactions and digital payments. Patil — with access to banking and a cell phone — could, in theory, move to cashless transactions, but in reality there is no Internet access and the government has . . . placed restrictions on . . . the cooperative bank [the NDCC] that hosts his account. [The government is afraid the NDCC, a co-op, might become a black-market bank.]

"Patil deposited Rs 21,000 by cheque in his NDCC account, hoping he could withdraw some money to pay labourers who work on his farm . . . [these are] transactions that still take place in cash . . . 'It takes more than two weeks for the cheque to be deposited,' said Patil.

" 'I have to stand in line at the bank from 10 am to 6 pm, and all I get is one Rs 2,000 note,' said Patil . . . He needed Rs 4,500 to pay labourers and Rs 4,000 for the mini truck that carries his produce to the market.

" 'Seventy percent of farmers in Nashik district have their accounts with NDCC,' said Shirish Kotwal . . . of NDCC.

"There were no [onion] auctions for ten days after [Modi's] demonetisation because of a lack of valid notes [i.e. cash] in the market. Onions stored in the market stayed unsold and when markets reopened, new produce flooded the market reducing onion prices.

"Onions, which were sold for Rs 1,000-1,200 per quintal (100 kg) in the weeks before *notebandi*, are now sold for Rs 600-700 per quintal.

"Patil, who owns four acres of land which he farms with his brothers, has made a loss of Rs 30,000 because of low onion prices."

My Reaction: SMH. This is modern-day finance in action. In the computer age. Administered by university-trained economists. Farmers would have done better.

Stock-Picking Strategy

There's a British stock-market proverb dating back 300 years that says: *Sell in May and go away. Stay away until St. Leger's Day*. St. Leger's Day was the last horse race of the season. It occurred each year in September.

Surprisingly, that adage still holds true in the USA today. Backtesting shows the best time to buy stocks is September 1st and the best time to sell those same stocks is the following May 15.

If you had used a buy-and-hold strategy, buying the DOW on September 1, 2006 and selling it 11½ years later on May 15, 2017, your overall gain would have been 117%.

But if you'd bought-and-sold, then bought-and-sold again — i.e. if you bought on September 1, then sold on May 15, then held cash for 3½ months, then repurchased stocks on September 1 — repeat, repeat, repeat — your gain would have been 142% over the same 11½ years.

But you can do better than that. Just pick stocks that beat the DOW. Easy peasy.

There are several "stock screeners" online — the *Yahoo! Stock Screener* and *Zachs Stock Screener* and the *Finiz Stock Screener* to name a few. The stock screeners tell you to select and quantify a criterion. Then they filter or screen out all the stocks that don't meet your threshold for the characteristic in question. Following is what I look for in a stock —

• I want a company's *total revenue* to be higher this year than last. That means business is booming; more money came through the front door this year.

• And I want a company's _net_ *income* to be a higher percent of the total revenue this year than it was last year. Don't just bring in more money; keep a higher percentage of it at home.

• I also look for stocks that are priced 50% higher today than they were last year. I want stocks that are on the way up. A higher price means that investors have noticed.

• And lastly, despite all the good news (bigger income, up 50%), I want a stock that is still undervalued. I want the company's Price/Sales Ratio or PSR to be <1 (under 1.0). PSR is a measure of value — similar to P/E but better. The book *Super Stocks* by Kenneth Fisher (you can buy it on Amazon) explains PSR.

But that's it. Once you've mastered a stock screener and the navigation of online financial pages, you'll be able to whittle down a universe of 20,000 stocks to a dozen good ones in half an hour. I've purchased stocks in everything from Israeli grocery stores to US-based airlines to companies that made wedding gowns. My gains have averaged 20% to 30% per year. All based strictly on the numbers; on the fundamentals; all based on "sell in May and go away . . ."

• *TIP.* If you try this strategy, real-time, then I suggest you only do it on paper for the first year or two. Don't buy anything. Using the criteria outlined above, pick out some stocks on September 1st, write down their prices, and see how they're doing the following May 15th. After you get comfortable with how well the strategy works, that's time enough to put your own hard-earned money at risk.

There's almost always one or two duds hidden in with the good stuff that I've never been able to filter out in advance. (Though it did happen a couple of times — in 20 years — that every one of my picks made money.) To protect yourself against the duds, buy everything on the list in equal measure.

I fully intended to share with you the actual results achieved from using this strategy. And I know with certainty that I filed the results away on my computer. Or on a thumb drive. Or somewhere . . . where they would never, ever be lost. Turns out my filing system is great but my retrieval system leaves something to be desired. As they say, #%*@#x!!

I was able — after some hair-tearing and bad language — to locate the results from seven different September-May holding periods scattered between 2008 and 2018. Those seven holding periods saw an average gain, using my picking system, of 29% per period. For comparison, the DOW achieved average gains of 6% per period (over those exact same periods).

Note that 2008 was a rough go. The DOW lost money and so did my picks. And those losses are included in the averages for the seven periods just cited, both for my picks (up 29%) and the DOW (up 6%).

But let's don't get too cocky, shall we? In 2018 I bought eleven stocks on September 3. As of May 15, 2019, nine of my 11 picks had lost money — handing me an overall loss of 15%. But the DOW was down less than 1% for the same period. I was astounded. I'd been doing this for 20 years and this had never happened before. *The DOW beat me?* Holy Mother of Pearl!

Foreign Bank Accounts

The most compelling reason to have a foreign bank account is because, in a fiscal crisis, governments install "capital controls" and forbid their citizens from moving domestic currency offshore. So a foreign bank account is a play-it-safe strategy for ordinary citizens.

To be effective — from the government's point of view — capital controls must be sprung upon an unsuspecting public before anyone has time to protect themselves. That means a foreign bank account is something you must establish ahead of time. Canadian dollars in a Canadian bank, for example, are largely beyond the grasp of U.S. authorities (unless you have a court judgement against you).

But why do you need money offshore? Consider this 2016 article from *The Guardian*:

"Bartering with strangers for leftover prescription drugs in Venezuela has become . . . commonplace . . . 'We found the [foreign-made] heart disease drug Manidon, which my mum takes daily, using WhatsApp. We [recently] bartered the drug for four rolls of toilet paper,' says Carlos Gonzalez, 35 . . . 'When my mother sees her stock of drugs declining, she starts cutting the pills and taking half a dose. If we can't find the medicines, there's nothing we can do.

We can't order over the internet *because we can't transfer funds abroad.*' " [emphasis added]

You'll have minimal reporting issues with the IRS if you keep your foreign account balance below $10,000. And $10,000 is a *total* figure; the sum of *all* foreign accounts over which you have signature authority. Anything greater than that means you must file FinCEN Form 114, Report of Foreign Bank and Financial Accounts (FBAR) along with your income tax. Probably you don't want to go there.

You may be able to set up a foreign account in your own name but, today, I wouldn't want to bet on it. You'll probably have to resort to a trusted friend or relative (already living in a foreign country) to set up an account for you — an account for you to use but over which only your friend has signature authority. I did say *trusted* friend, didn't I? But the "trusted-friend method" does sidestep the $10,000 restriction. That's a plus.

I, personally, lucked out when I accepted a job in Toronto some years ago. It was completely on the up-and-up. I lived in Canada with a Canadian address and was enrolled in the Canadian health care system (they have socialized medicine). I paid Canadian income tax and not U.S. income tax. A government agency in Ottawa — operating by treaty with the U.S. — reviewed my application and determined that, for tax purposes, I was officially a Canadian person and not a U.S. person. My Canadian paycheck in Canadian dollars from my Canadian company was direct-deposited into my Canadian checking account. Upon retirement I returned to the states but left the checking account open.

Today, my monthly SIN stipend (the equivalent of U.S. Social Security) is direct-deposited in Canadian dollars to that same Canadian checking account.

But how do I deposit additional money into that account? The bank building is not just down the street anymore. And how about you? Now that you have a foreign account that you can use, opened in your behalf by a foreign friend, say, how do you make a deposit? This can be difficult info to come by. So let me share some possibilities —

• Wire transfer. International wire transfers have been around for a long time and are the most secure (but also the most expensive) means of transferring money. Your bank will arrange it; just ask at the teller's window. International wire transfer fees range from $17.50 to $50 per transaction. Plus the banks gouge a bit on the exchange rate.

The preceding paragraph perhaps conveys the impression that wire transfers, although expensive, are foolproof. Let me clarify that with a personal story. Years ago, my bride-to-be was in the Philippines and I wanted her to have some extra cash in her pocket when she traveled to the USA (to marry me, lucky girl). So I wire-transferred money from my U.S. bank account to her Philippine bank account.

She went to her bank daily to check the status and always got the runaround. It had arrived and was in the building, yes, but it was always on another floor or in another department being checked out for this or that. After my fiancée left for the states, her sister took up the cause and visited the bank daily. Several weeks went by and I finally mentioned it to my U.S. bank. "That's ridiculous," they said. "We'll cancel it." So I got my money back less the nonrefundable transfer fee.

A couple of years later we vacationed in the Philippines and saw President Ramos on TV making a pitch to potential foreign investors. "Don't forget us," he admonished. "Don't forget our potential. Invest here . . ."

Say what? I can't trust you guys with hundreds so now I should trust you with thousands? Really?

• Personal check. The easiest way (not the cheapest or fastest) for me to transfer funds from my New York State bank to my Canadian account is to write a personal check. My New York State bank instructed me on the correct way to do it —

Write the check to *yourself* (i.e. "Pay to the order of . . . your own name). Do not make it out to "cash" or to the name of the foreign bank. Writing "U.S. dollars" or "USD" on the face of the check is not necessary; the currency type is defaulted to the parent currency of the bank on which the check is drawn. Sign the front of the check (meaning it's written "to" yourself and is authorized by yourself). Then endorse the back of the check with your signature and write, "For deposit only to Marine Midland (i.e. the bank name) Account No. 1234567." So your name and/or signature appears three times — twice on the front and once on the back.

Don't forget to include a deposit slip. Personally, I do write "USD" on the deposit slip. When received by the Canadian bank, my deposit in U.S. dollars is converted to Canadian dollars and deposited. It can take (by law) up to 30 days for the transaction although most banks waive the time allowance.

As an experiment, on December 27, 2016 I mailed a $100 deposit to my Canadian checking account via a personal check drawn on my NYS bank account. The postage stamp was $1.15.

Sixteen days later, on January 12, 2017, the Canadian bank credited my account with $123.82 Canadian dollars — an exchange rate of 1.2382. According to exchangerates.org, the exchange rate on January 12 was 1.3151. https://www.exchangerates.org.uk/USD-CAD-spot-exchange-rates-history-2017.html

So they nicked me for 6% on the exchange-rate.

● There are many commercial companies (e.g. Western Union, TransferWise, CurrencyFair, Moneygram, OFX, and many more) that will do international transfers for you.

TransferWise looks to be the least expensive. Their fee is half a percent to send $US 1,000 (less for larger amounts). Their conversion rate is the midpoint between bid and ask. The transaction takes one business day. https://transferwise.com/us?ircid=3512&utm_campaign=Nerdwallet+&utm_source=Nerdwallet%2C+Inc&utm_medium=affiliate

You'll have to open an account and establish your identity. A jpg copy of your passport emailed to them will do that. But this means you can't wait until the last minute to make a deposit. Just initializing an account with TransferWise may take a few days.

And, depending on the service you use (TransferWise or somebody else) you may have to tell them the passwords of your bank accounts. After all, they have to be able to get into your account to take money out to send someplace. If you're not comfortable with that, well, it's back to face-to-face cash and personal checks and wire transfers.

And you'll need to understand "transit numbers." The funny-looking numbers on the bottom of your personal checks (called MICR or Magnetic Ink Character Recognition code) contain (in the U.S.) a bank routing number and your account number. But TransferWise and similar ask for your "transit number." What the heck is that and where do you find it?

Turns out the MICR Code along the bottom of my *Canadian* check is formatted thusly —

1001 : 12345 : 678 : 9876543210

> *1001* is the Check number
> *12345* is the 5-digit **Transit number**
> *678* is the 3-digit Financial Institution number
> *9876543210* is the Account number (up to 12 digits)

And the MICR Code on my *American* check is formatted differently —

067812345 : 9876543210 : 1001

> *067812345* is the **Routing number**
> > *0* is a leading zero (a constant) at the beginning of the 9-digit routing number
> > *678* is the 3-digit Financial Institution number within the 9-digit routing number
> > *12345* is the 5-digit **Transit number** within the 9-digit routing number
> *9876543210* is the Account number
> *1001* is the Check number

- PayPal. I have a U.S. PayPal account, a U.S. bank account, and a Canadian bank account. I can, with a few keystrokes, transfer funds from PayPal to my U.S. bank account at no charge. But I cannot transfer money from my U.S. PayPal account to my Canadian bank account. There's a conflict between the 9-digit U.S. routing number and the 8-digit Canadian combo of Transit-Number-plus-Financial-Institution.

It appears that my best way to transfer funds from PayPal to my Canadian bank — not bank-to-bank but PayPal-to-bank (*international* bank) — is to use Xoom, a transfer service owned by PayPal. It's more expensive than TransferWise but Xoom guarantees your funds will transfer successfully. https://www.xoom.com/money-transfer

- Abra. An app called Abra appeared in 2017. It was developed and debugged USA-to-Philippines. But today, in 2021, Abra appears to be worldwide. With Abra, you have a bitcoin-type wallet on your smartphone and can transfer money from your U.S. bank account to that wallet. You can then transfer money from your wallet to a foreign bank account. Behind the scenes, invisible to the user, are two steps wherein funds are converted dollars-to-bitcoin and, later, again converted bitcoins-to-local currency (pesos in the case of the Philippines).

Today, Abra's 2021 webpage says you can add money to your wallet using a bank account, credit or debit card, cash, bitcoin, ether, litecoin, etc. You can use any of 117 cryptocurrencies and 54 fiat currencies, all from one app. https://www.abra.com/

Does Abra work in Venezuela? In 2019 the answer was *yes*:

"We recently caught up with researcher Alejandro Machado, who spent part of 2018 investigating how people are using cryptocurrencies in Venezuela.

" 'If you want to send money to someone in Venezuela,' Machado says, 'An app like Abra can become your bank . . . If I go through the Abra network, I could send money to my friend's [Abra] account [in Venezuela] and he could use it selectively, keep it in dollars, and only use whatever necessary.' " https://www.abra.com/blog/bitcoin-and-bolivars/

But today (starting May 2021), the answer is *maybe*. Today, Abra requires customers in 43 countries plus one state (New York) fill out a "Global KYC" (Know Your Customer) application. It really startled me to find New York State on the same list as Venezuela, North Korea, and Afghanistan. Really? New York State is where *I* live. What the heck is goin' on here?

To summarize, please remember that just having a foreign bank account, or access to a foreign account, is not enough. You need to know how to use it. Experiment. Make a deposit using a personal check. Try Abra. Try Xoom. Do a wire transfer. Admittedly, it costs some time and a few dollars. But you need to *know*, before your day of desperation arrives, what works and what doesn't.

Bitcoin

"I just don't get it," people say. "Can you explain bitcoin to me? How does it work? And it's not backed by anything. How can you place value on something like that?"

72

A big part of the problem is familiarity. U.S. dollars aren't backed by anything either. But we spend them and accept them every day. If you had a yard sale and somebody offered you pesos or Euros or yen . . . would you accept them? Would you trust them? It's much the same thing.

Warren Buffet is a famous billionaire investor. And he advises, "Never invest in a business you cannot understand." I agree. Then again, how much understanding do we need?

Computers operate on a binary number system (zeros and ones). Do your grandchildren understand binary? If not, how can they use the internet? How about Ohm's law in electricity ($I = V \div R$)? Do your grandkids understand that? If not, then how can they flip on the electric light bulb over the kitchen sink?

So how much understanding must we have of bitcoin methodology — blockchain, distributed ledgers, mining, private keys, hard forks, etc. — before we can use it effectively?

True, I am cautious. Cryptocurrency technology is new and is still in a shakedown phase. It has not earned blind trust. In 2014, for example, the bitcoin exchange Mt. Gox in Japan was hacked for $460 million.
https://www.wired.com/2014/03/bitcoin-exchange/

In 2018, the Japanese exchange Coincheck suffered an attack costing $534 million in NEM coins (New Economy Movement). https://www.investopedia.com/news/largest-cryptocurrency-hacks-so-far-year/

BitConnect, *PlusToken*, and *Pincoin* are all crypto Ponzi schemes and frauds that deceived thousands of investors, bilking them, in total, of some $5 billion since 2018.

In 2021, hackers stole $611 million in ethereum by breaching the blockchain-based platform Poly Network. https://www.indiatoday.in/technology/news/story/hackers-steal-611-million-in-ethereum-and-other-cryptocurrencies-in-largest-defi-crypto-theft-1839408-2021-08-11

As of August 31, "The number of cases of cryptocurrency breaches and fraud is on track to break records in 2021; 32 incidents of hacks and fraud for a total value of $2.99 billion have taken place so far in 2021." https://markets.businessinsider.com/news/currencies/cryptocurrency-hacks-fraud-cases-record-bitcoin-ethereum-wallets-breaches-defi-2021-8

Volatility is another problem. Bitcoin is a poor "store of value." In the six weeks before Christmas 2017, the price of bitcoin went up 138%. You could have doubled your money in six weeks.

But in the following ten weeks (from Christmas 2017 to April 2018) it went down 54%. That, my friend, will wear out the batteries in your pacemaker PDQ.

However, though not a reliable *store of value*, bitcoins are excellent as a means of *transferring* wealth, moving it across borders and around the world with minimal government interference. Let's walk through an example showing the mechanics of how the transfer function operates.

There are really two scenarios. One is sending money *into* an area already infected with extreme inflation (sending

74

money into Venezuela today). That's where Abra, described earlier, has proven itself.

The other scenario is sending money *out of* a troubled country to preserve buying power before things go more to hell than they already have. That would be the situation in Venezuela a few years ago. Say you'd been working in the Venezuelan oil fields, saving your pennies, and the government was starting to restrict you from taking those savings out of the country. You, on the other hand, want to get your savings out while they're still worth something. That's where bitcoin can help.

What follows is a description of the second scenario. I've decided to use the USA and Canada in this example and steer clear of Venezuela. I just want to explain the mechanics of how it works.

So . . . let's say you live and work in the USA and you foresee runaway inflation and government restrictions on the horizon. And you want get some money out of the U.S. (while you still can) and into Canada (which you view as a safe haven). And you're going to use bitcoin to do it.

First, you need a USA bank account with some money in it. (That might be the hardest part of all.) Your U.S. account will be denominated in U.S. dollars.

Next you need a smartphone. And you need a "hot wallet" on your smartphone. It's an app. "Hot wallets" are connected to the internet. *Coinbase* is one brand of hot wallet that supports "bitcoin." (Bitcoin, itself, is a brand of cryptocurrency albeit the first and the biggest. Not all wallets support all brands of crypto).

Then you need an account with an "exchange" that supports the bitcoin brand. (In this context the word *exchange* is a noun and is used in much the same sense as it appears in the phrase New York Stock Exchange.) If you Google for "bitcoin exchange" you'll locate several USA exchanges, all just a click away. https://www.bitcoin.com/bitcoin-exchange-directory

Coinbase (the hot-wallet brand mentioned above) is also a bitcoin exchange. *Coinbase* boasts that it is "the easiest place to buy bitcoin."

So let's say you elect to use bitcoin (brand) cryptocurrency (and not litecoin or dash or ethereum, etc.). You're sending money out of the USA and you've decided (on the USA end of things) to use *Coinbase* as both your wallet and your exchange.

Next, you need a destination for your money. In this example it means you need a friend in Canada who, like yourself, has a smartphone and a wallet and an account with a bitcoin exchange. (It need not be the same "brand" of wallet or exchange as what you employ. You're using *Coinbase* as both wallet-and-exchange; your friend might use, say, *Exodus* — also a combo wallet-and-exchange.)

And, lastly, you need a Canadian bank account. Or the use of a Canadian bank account. It's nearly impossible, today, for a U.S. citizen to open a foreign bank account. But your destination account can be in someone else's name. And that's perhaps a good thing.

So, to transfer funds, the sequence is this. First, you authorize *Coinbase* to withdraw some U.S. dollars from your U.S. bank account.

76

Coinbase makes the withdrawal and you now have U.S. dollars on deposit with *Coinbase.* Next you instruct *Coinbase* to buy bitcoins with those dollars. Then you transfer the bitcoins from the exchange to your personal wallet and send them to your friend's wallet in Canada. It's like making a phone call.

Let's say the U.S. government has forbidden its citizens to send U.S. dollars out of the country. Ah! But you're not sending dollars. You're sending bitcoins.

On the Canadian end, your friend receives the bitcoins into his wallet and uses them (via his *Exodus* exchange) to buy Canadian dollars. Lastly, using *Exodus*, he deposits the Canadian dollars into the agreed-upon Canadian bank account. This effectively puts your money beyond the reach of your home government — it's in a foreign currency in a foreign bank in somebody else's name.

How long does this take? Well, overall, from the time you tell *Coinbase* to withdraw some U.S. dollars from your U.S. bank until those same funds are deposited in Canadian dollars in a Canadian bank, some 20 minutes will have elapsed (on a good day). On an average day, more like two hours. But two days (or even more) isn't out of the question.

How does that compare? Well, it took 16 days (if you recall from a previous section) for me to transfer money from my U.S. bank account to my Canadian bank account via personal check. And the law allows the banks 30 days to make the transfer).

A bank-to-bank wire transfer (international) takes from one to five days plus a stiff transaction fee.

Back to our example. Once your funds are on the Canadian side of the border, don't let your friend leave the digital money on deposit with the *Exodus* exchange. In the ethereum hack of June 2016, anyone who had been lazy and left their "digital money" in their "brokerage account" at the exchange (instead of moving it to a personal hot wallet on their smartphone) had 36% of their funds "appropriated" to reimburse other customers/victims who had suffered a loss at the hands of hackers. It was a bail-in — just like Cyprus.

Hacks are to cryptocurrency as counterfeiting is to printed money. Both are rare but neither one is likely to go away anytime soon. As consumers and users, we need — in both cases — to display reasonable caution so as to minimize our risks.

Hot wallets are connected to the internet. A further security step (optional) is a "cold wallet." There are different kinds of cold wallets. The safest is a "hardware" cold wallet. A hardware wallet is a physical device that is stored offline but can be plugged into a computer when needed. Hardware wallets are essentially hacker-proof. *Trezor* is one brand. In use, you would keep a small amount of funds in your hot wallet for day-to-day transactions but the bulk of your wealth would be in an off-line cold wallet for safekeeping.

Now, why bother with all this? It seems like we'll invest a lot of time and trouble to set up hot wallets and cold wallets and bitcoin exchange accounts. Why not just use Western Union? It would be a lot simpler, no?

Venezuela holds at least part of the answer: "Remittance processors like . . . Western Union closed operations in Venezuela [in 2005, 16 years ago] when the government enacted various sanctions against them . . ." https://news.bitcoin.com/venezuelan-brokerage-cryptobuyer-demand/

However, today (2021) it appears Western Union can again be used to send U.S. dollars *into* Venezuela. https://www.westernunion.com/ve/en/home.html

On the other hand, if you want to transfer money (bolivars) *out* of Venezuela, be prepared to snuggle up next to your computer for a long evening of searching as you try to figure out *how*. And that's where bitcoin can help. Because bitcoin is *not money*.

Well . . . then again, maybe it is. El Salvador recently decided to accept bitcoin as legal tender. After 9/7/2021, businesses will be obliged to accept bitcoin as payment. https://www.bbc.com/news/technology-58473260

As if that weren't enough, on 9/28/2021 El Salvador "mined 0.00599179 bitcoin, or about $269 worth, with power harnessed from a volcano." https://www.cnbc.com

Ain't technology grand?

But back to Venezuela. Things got rather messy there. Before 2017 you could have used the *Surbitcoin* exchange to send your bitcoins out of Venezuela. But in 2017 *Surbitcoin's* bank (Banesco), under government pressure, closed *Surbitcoin's* account. There were workarounds but it was a long and winding road.

It's fair to say that, in Venezuela, cryptocurrency became a challenge to use (due to government meddling). But, while crypto was difficult, Western Union was *impossible*; it no longer existed. The takeaway is that, difficult or not, *transferring* funds from one account or country to another is where cryptocurrency excels.

On the downside, crypto is *not* a good store of value. The week-to-week price variation is just too unpredictable — save $1000 this week in bitcoin and next week you might just have $500.

> • **TIP.** Keep in mind that, if you buy something and pay for it using crypto, then what you've done, in effect, is to have *sold* crypto. And if you come out ahead on the trade, any profit you make is taxable income. The U.S. government takes the view that, for U.S. citizens, it doesn't matter *where* a gain is realized (i.e. in what country your trade took place). Your profit is taxable in the U.S.

If your inner geek really, really wants to know how cryptocurrency works, then *Dash,* another brand of cryptocurrency, has an excellent series of YouTube tutorials explaining the nuts-and-bolts of how everything functions. (Dash, incidentally, is a portmanteau of Digital and Cash.)

I suggest viewing the first three Dash videos (listed below). For a half-hour investment of time you'll begin to understand how crypto works. (The operative word is *begin*.)

- *What Is a Blockchain?* | *DASH School #1* [8-minute video] https://www.youtube.com/watch?v=e7UwwcCKj4Y

- *How Does a Blockchain Work?* | *DASH School #2* [8-minute video] https://www.youtube.com/watch?v=eS39N-mHrOs

- *How Can a Blockchain be a Monetary System?* | *DASH School #3* [8-minute video] https://www.youtube.com/watch?annotation_id=annotation_2147100541&feature=iv&src_vid=e7UwwcCKj4Y&v=DyywtVNlfFs

"Is bitcoin a company?" I've been asked that question.

And the answer is, "No. Bitcoin is not a company." Nor is bitcoin owned by any company. Nor does bitcoin represent shares in a company. In fact, Wikipedia says that bitcoin does not even have a "central authority." (But who decided that? A central authority?)

The supply of bitcoins in the world is increased via "mining." The miners use computers to solve riddles (for lack of a better term). The first miner to solve a riddle is rewarded with a brand new bitcoin (or fraction thereof) created out of thin air. Then all the miners move on to the next riddle. Each riddle is progressively harder to solve than its predecessor. So crypto mining requires ever-bigger computers plus more and more electricity to run the computers.

As of November 2021, 18.8 million bitcoins had been mined. The ultimate supply is limited to 21 million. But who decided that? And who might try to change it? And

81

who is it that will enforce the 21-million rule? There is no central authority, remember?

I've long been of the opinion that cryptocurrency would only succeed until it posed a competitive threat to some form or other of government-issued money. Then it would be banned. But the fact that *mining* crypto consumes an ever-increasing amount of electricity might turn out to be an even bigger issue.

"At this point [June 2021], the Bitcoin network consumes about 116 terawatt hours, or 116 trillion watts per year. That's about 0.5% of the total electricity in the world — more electricity consumption than in many countries." https://www.etftrends.com/2021/06/why-is-bitcoin-mining-so-energy-intensive/

China made cryptocurrency illegal in 2021. All crypto mining and crypto transactions were banned. Financial institutions (banks) were forbidden from providing any service related to cryptocurrency. Overseas crypto exchanges were barred from providing services to China-based investors.

There were two reasons for China's action. For one thing, private cryptocurrency potentially poses a threat to China's upcoming government-issued, digital-yuan (which is in an advanced pilot stage). But crypto mining also consumes electricity. And China, as we speak, is hurting energy-wise. Brownouts and blackouts are common this year. China may have been the first country to outlaw crypto but I daresay it won't be the last.

Overall, as an investor, I see four weaknesses with crypto as a portfolio holding.

(1) It can be banned by a government at the stroke of a pen. As China has done.

(2) "No internet" equates to "no crypto." With no internet, having a stash of bitcoin in an offline hardware wallet would be like having a stash of paper dollars in a foreign safety deposit box with Covid travel restrictions in place. Yeah, you own it. It's there. Safe and sound. But you can't get to it. Just like crypto with no internet.

The internet could crash — more like be *smashed* — due to war. How many missiles and torpedoes would be required to take out the key servers and fiber optic cables? Their locations are not exactly secret. You can find maps online. Crypto is useless without the internet.

(3) But we don't need a war. Sooner or later, statistically speaking, it is a certainty that the internet will fail due to natural causes — sunspots, for example — like the Carrington Event of 1859 during solar cycle 10.

(4) And lastly, today's "crypto mania" resembles (to my eye) the Dutch "tulip mania" of the 1600's. Are you familiar with *Extraordinary Popular Delusions and the Madness of Crowds* by Charles Mackay, 1841? At its peak, *one* Viceroy Tulip bulb sold for ten times the annual salary of a skilled laborer. It shouldn't surprise anyone that tulip investors lost a lot of money in the collapse that followed. It was a classic example of *normalcy bias* and *lineal thinking*.

For comparison, in the USA today, an experienced truck driver can earn $80,000 per year. Ten times that amount would be $800,000.

"A panel of 50 bitcoin and cryptocurrency experts has predicted the bitcoin price will continue to climb through 2021, hitting highs of around $80,000, before surging to $250,000 by 2025 and a staggering $5 million per bitcoin by 2030." — Billy Bambrough for *Forbes*, Oct. 23, 2021

On November 8, 2021, one bitcoin traded for $68,000. High enough to make me squirm.

The Backing for Money is Debt

Say you want to buy a car. You find one that you like for $30,000. They'll take your old car as a trade-in for $10,000. That means you'll have to finance $20,000.

You go to your bank and fill out a loan application. They call the next day and say your loan has been approved. You go in to sign the papers. The bank officer hands you a certified check for $20,000. You walk to the teller's window and deposit it in your checking account. Your next stop is the car dealer.

That $20,000 — whether you realize it or not — is brand new money, just created out of thin air. It didn't exist yesterday. No printed greenbacks were used in the transaction. No gold was shuffled around in the bank's vault.

Your credit rating — your track record of on-time loan repayment — played a big role in the loan being approved; in the new money being created. Your promise to repay the $20,000 . . . and the bank's opinion that you are trustworthy . . . is the only backing that exists for that money.

So you stop by and pay the car dealer. He later pays his mechanics using the money that you borrowed. The money supply of the USA was increased by $20,000 based on your newly acquired *debt*. That's what backs our entire money system. Debt.

The Chicago Plan

In these perplexing times, when researching the economy, you'll sometimes see reference to the Chicago Plan. In reverential tones. As if it's the answer to everything. But what is it? What was it?

"The Chicago plan was a collection of banking reforms suggested by University of Chicago economists in the wake of the Great Depression. A six-page memorandum on banking reform was given limited and confidential distribution to about forty individuals on 16 March 1933." — Wikipedia

> IMF Working Paper: *The Chicago Plan Revisited* by Jaromir Benes and Michael Kumhof, 2012, 69 pages, says: "The Chicago Plan provides an outline for the transition of privately-issued debt-based money to a system of government-issued debt-free money." (page 18) https://www.imf.org/external/pubs/ft/wp/2012/wp12202.pdf

Note the IMF Working Paper confirms that today's backing for money is debt.

But we already knew that. The fundamental thrust of the Chicago Plan is to take the creation of money away from the private bankers and give it to the government. That's the essence of the proposal. That's the point to the whole thing. But to figure that out, simple as it may be, you must shovel your way through a serious pile of convoluted verbal bullshit.

> ASIDE. Forgive my little rant here BUT . . . The Gunning Fog Index is a test of readability. A Fog Index score of "8" means something is written on the 8th grade level. A score of "13" means it's written on a college Freshman level. My own writing is typically between Junior High and High School level. The IMF Working Paper referenced above is written on the "28.4" grade level. There ain't no such thing.

Back to the topic at hand. The Federal Reserve, despite its name, is a private group, not elected. The Federal Reserve a.k.a. "the Fed" serves as the U.S. central bank. Today, the Fed plus your neighborhood bank jointly control the money supply. The Chicago Plan was based on the unspoken premise that private bankers are something less than honest whereas the government — drumroll, please — is trustworthy.

And that may be. But the pathway to hell is paved with good intentions. If you really want to mess things up, IMHO, get the government involved. Remember the Ronald Reagan quote? "The nine most terrifying words in the English language are: *I'm from the government and I'm here to help.*"

So . . . Fed? . . . or government? . . . that's the choice, yes? *No! Not quite.* It's the Fed that exists today. On a personal basis, what we need to do is understand the system as it really operates today and figure out how best to live with it (or in spite of it).

My fear is this. The Chicago Plan will take money creation away from the people who know what they're doing (the private sector — people who may be crooked or dishonest but who at least understand the mechanics of what they're doing) and transfer money creation to (equally crooked or dishonest) government officials who *don't* know what they're doing; who don't understand the mechanics or consequences of what they're doing.

Are my fears ill-founded? Consider. Roosevelt forbade U.S. citizens to own gold in 1933. Just two years later, in 1935, Gerald Ford (later President Ford) graduated from the University of Michigan. He had majored in economics and political science. Ford then obtained a law degree from Yale and later spent 24 years in the House of Representatives.

The prohibition against owning gold was partially lifted by President Ford on December 31, 1974 and completely lifted by Congress in 1977.
https://www.wikiwand.com/en/Executive_Order_6102

BUT . . . earlier in 1974 Ford saw investment advisor Jim Blanchard (whose memoir was entitled *Confessions of a Gold Bug*) on TV raise a bar of gold and ask, "Why can I not own this?" Ford, 61 years old at that time and President of the United States, did not know when he saw Blanchard that it was a federal crime to own gold. Say what?
http://www.huffingtonpost.com/steve-mariotti/when-owning-gold-was-ille_b_10708196.html

How could he not have known? Even *I* knew that. Lord, have mercy on our souls.

Compound Interest

We all remember the childhood narrative about doubling a penny every day for a month. A penny isn't much to start with but it turns into a million dollars on day 28.

The penny story is really an example of compound interest. It's just that the interest rate is 100%. And it's not 100% per year; it's 100% *per day*.

A lower interest rate over a longer period of time (20% per year, say, instead of 100% per *day*) would stretch out the time between doublings (from 24 hours to 4 years) but would not prevent doubling. At 3% per year, doubling only occurs after a couple of decades (24 years to be exact).

Point is, be it fast or be it slow, infinite periodic doubling is impossible. The population of the U.S. has been compounding by a little over 1% per year. Doesn't sound like much but it can't go on forever. After the population of earth doubles enough times there will only be one square foot of land left per person. Later on, the weight of people on the earth will equal the weight of the earth. Simple arithmetic.

But we all ignore the simple arithmetic. We all ignore the inevitable. Can you name one car dealer or city government or corporation that does not aspire to year-over-year *perpetual growth*. Yet it cannot be.

The U.S. Patent Office will not entertain patent applications for perpetual motion machines. But all governments worldwide espouse endless *economic* growth as a worthy goal. It cannot be. Endless growth (or *attempted* endless growth) leads to collapse. Every time. Every. Single. Time.

Inflation, Deflation or Gridlock . . . That is the Question

Here's where the rubber meets the road.

The modern-day business cycle rhymes, if you will, with inflation-depression-inflation-depression. And so it has been for the 582 years starting with Gutenberg's printing press in 1439. 'Cause you won't have much printed paper money if you didn't have a press to print it with.

Inflation is an increase in the money supply. It is characterized by higher prices. When the current money supply is diluted with new money, each dollar is worth less than before. When dollars are worth less, goods are worth more (in dollar terms) and prices go up.

Depression (or "deflation") is the opposite. When the money supply shrinks there are less dollars in circulation than before. Money is more scarce, more valuable. More valuable money means that prices go *down*. Depressions are characterized by lower business activity, higher unemployment, and lower prices.

It would appear on the surface that, with printing-press money, not constrained by gold or silver, *deflation* is all but impossible. The government can prevent *that* from happening by just revving up the presses. Right?

Wrong. Because our money supply consists of more than just printed currency —

> "[Author Yuval Noah] Harari describes money as a 'collective fiction.' He notes that the total value of money worldwide is $60 trillion dollars, of which a

mere $6 trillion is in cash or coins. This means 90% of all money is nothing more than entries in a computer server. Money, says Harari, is a 'faith-based object,' whose value is derived by the shared narrative about its worth."

https://www.ngpf.org/blog/uncategorized/question-percentage-money-supply-physical-coins-currency/

Gee. Sounds more like bitcoin all the time.

Most of our money supply is in the form of checking account balances. It is debt-based money, created when a bank makes a loan.

The Fed can create an easy-money policy but it cannot force people to go in debt. Therein lies the rub. The Fed's power to increase the money supply is limited by the willingness of individuals to go in debt. As Paul Samuelson puts it in *Economics* (a standard college text for lo! these many years), "This is summarized by the aphorism 'the central bank can pull on a string (to curb booms) but it can't *push on a string* (to reverse deep slumps).' "

A depression is a shrinkage or contraction of the money supply. But the roots of depression, ironically, are found in *inflation*. The sequence — our traditional *business cycle* — is this. First, the money supply is inflated. Then, when the inflation is recognized, investors demand higher interest rates to keep ahead of it. They enforce their demand and obtain those higher rates by paying less for bonds.

The government doesn't set bond interest rates. Buyers set the rates by bidding against each other.

A higher bond interest rate results from higher inflation. Then the higher bond rate is piled on top of the inflation. The consumer sees not just higher prices at the grocery store but higher interest rates when he borrows — *guaranteeing* that loans will not be repaid. At some point they *cannot* be repaid due to the nature of simple arithmetic and compound interest. They will be defaulted and the money supply will collapse. Inflation is the straw that breaks the camel's back. Inflation is what propels us into depression.

"Fiscal policy" addresses taxation and government spending and is controlled by legislation. "Monetary policy" is concerned with interest rates and money supply and is controlled by the Fed. Monetary policy is what's used to control inflation and deflation.

When banks get in trouble, they expect the Fed to come to their rescue. And one way the Fed can get more money (more purchasing power) in the banks' hands is through *deflation*. Deflation — shrinking the money supply — makes the money that the banks already hold more valuable. And it's the banks that the Fed is chartered to protect and enrich, not you and I.

So, even though we're all watching consumer prices go up at the moment and fretting about inflation (or even the likelihood of runaway inflation), *deflation* lurks in the shadows. I suggest you not write it off just yet.

But wait! This whole traditional "business cycle" thing assumes *positive* interest rates.

Today, with *negative* rates — something that's never been tried or tested before — I suspect that investors, observing inflation, and wanting higher rates to stay ahead of it, and being confronted with not just lower rates but with *negative* rates, might refuse to buy bonds.

They might turn to gold instead. Resulting in gold being outlawed. Resulting in much confusion and the whole system going into a tailspin . . .

The feelings of bond buyers will be akin to my own values about the merits of saving for a rainy day. The good feeling I have about *saving* implies positive rates. I won't struggle to save money for the joy of losing money. (But you're welcome to do so if that's what you want.)

Our government runs on borrowed money. It borrows more every year just to pay the interest on last year's borrowing. With negative rates, investors might refuse to buy bonds (because they'll lose money). That means they won't be lending money to the government — and the government will shut down. Or default. If the U.S. government defaults on its bonds — with Japan owning $1.2 trillion and China owning $1.1 trillion of U.S. government debt — then the whole system, worldwide, will crash and burn.

Maybe the Fed or the IMF or the Bank of International Settlements can devise a system whereby bank savers lose money but bond buyers make money. Ya think?

So what can we expect if the new, negative-rate money system gets a fart stuck crossways? What will we face in the breaking wind of a foul Fed collapse — inflation, deflation, or gridlock? Actually — from the point of view

92

of an individual citizen — in all three scenarios, *barter* will break its shackles and rule supreme once more. Call it the business cycle at low tide.

So What's the Best Barter Item?

How best to preserve your wealth is really the gist of this write-up. Can you imagine the day when hoarding tangible trade goods (whiskey, condoms, and canning jar lids) preserves your wealth better than a money market fund?

A barter economy, of course, necessitates haggling. No more will we amble around Walmart comparing price tags. The prices we pay for things will be subject to negotiation. And to be successful, that requires an understanding of body language. What does it mean when a buyer folds his arms across his chest? Or when the pupils of his eyes dilate? (That's why Chinese merchants wear dark glasses; so you can't see the dilation.)

Incidentally, just so you know, the 1991 book entitled *The Haggler's Handbook* by Koren and Goodman is available on Amazon and has the perfect title. But it's geared towards big-ticket items (cars and houses and factories) and not yard sales.

Story time. I once worked in Kuching, the capital of Sarawak, a state in Malaysia. Actually, Kuching is on the island of Borneo (Land of Headhunters). My wife was with me. I wanted to buy her some jewelry as a souvenir. Neither of us spoke Bahasa Melayu, the local language. A native woman, the mother of a young man I worked with in the office, offered to take us shopping. We went to a jewelry store. The jeweler was Chinese. The store faced a crowded, noisy, open-air street market. An electronic screen hung on the wall flashing, minute-by-minute, the current New York price of gold expressed in ringgit (the local currency). The atmosphere was festive. We picked out a necklace. The native woman haggled. After five minutes the price came down. Way down. My wife said, "Wow! We'll take it." The jeweler smiled. "Sold."

The native woman was not happy when we left the shop and started down the street. She was scowling. "I wasn't finished," she told us. "You paid way too much." She clearly felt we had wasted her time.

Having desirable barter items (like the ones listed below) will be essential in the barter economy that likely awaits us. But negotiating skills will be equally important. Can you imagine, here in the states, going to a jewelry store and bartering for a wedding ring?

"How about the ring in exchange for my painting the kitchen? Plus a bushel of potatoes."

"Okay . . . as long as you supply the paint."

But back to the barter items themselves. Here are the rules for good barter items (adapted from Joel Skousen's writings):

1. High demand. If no one wants it, no one wants it.
2. Difficult to manufacture on your own.
3. Durable for long-term storage.
4. Can be easily divided up into smaller quantities.
5. Authenticity and quality are easily recognizable.

And here's a list of barter goods you might consider — canning jars; sewing supplies (needles, thread, zippers, buttons, safety pins); road maps (for when everybody's GPS goes kaput); trash bags; leather gloves; children's shoes; matches & lighters; flashlight batteries; .22 shells; salt; sugar; coffee; tea; rice; chocolate; yeast; canned meat; powdered milk; small hand tools (hammers, pliers, screwdrivers); bicycle parts; gardening tools; bug spray; epoxy glue; off-the-shelf reading glasses; soap; toilet paper; children's cold medicine; toothache drops; painkillers; disposable razors & shaving cream; face masks (e.g. N95 masks); ladies' make-up, blankets . . .

But, instead of investing all our *money* in trade goods, perhaps we should invest some of our *time* (the most precious commodity of all) in learning barterable *skills* — midwifery, repairing musical instruments, making wine. In hard times, skills will serve us better than a stash of cash or a box of candles. Knowing how to *make* candles will put us further ahead than having a hoard of candles.

The guy with two kids and a house mortgage doesn't have much spare money to save or invest anyway. But he can pay his house mortgage while studying algebra . . . or learning to repair zippers. He *can* pay his house mortgage and acquire *skills* at the same time.

So here's a list of barterable skills (some from before the days of electricity and internal combustion engines) — making soap; home canning of vegetables and meat; gardening (knowing how to grow vegetables); growing onion sets or seed potatoes; auto & tractor repair; knowing how to file income tax returns; house painting; carpentry; dog training; hatching chicks; milking cows by hand; sheep shearing; cutting hay with a grass scythe; saving open-pollinated vegetable seeds; foraging for wild food; skinning and cleaning fish and game; grinding flour (by hand or powered with a treadmill); sewing (by hand or with an electric machine or with a treadle machine); darning socks; knitting (by hand and/or with a machine); cutting firewood; making barrel stoves; building Russian fireplaces; capturing energy (generators, windmills, solar panels, treadmills); eyeglass repair; building a privy; ammo reloading; riding shotgun or being a bodyguard; preparing houses to withstand attack; providing taxi service or trucking service; piloting (flying); driving (a car, tractor, horse); bike repair (pedal bikes, electric bikes, motor bikes, motorcycles, scooters); sending messages via shortwave radio; tutoring "new math"; teaching 3R's to children; teaching music; teaching dance; teaching drawing; advising on statistics; saw sharpening, setting-up and administering a barter club; barbering; babysitting; welding; locksmithing; small engine repair; building root cellars, barns, chicken coops; repairing electronics; shoe repair. Etcetera. Etcetera. Point is, barterable *skills* will keep you going a lot longer than barter *goods*.

The IRS can't tax your skills (your ability to speak Spanish or use Morse code or grade rare coins). And, unlike gold, you can cross international borders without fear of your skills/assets being confiscated. Plus, on either side of the border, skills have earning potential. *Say again.* Skills have earning potential.

What was it we said way back at the very beginning of this write-up? "The *intrinsic value* of a manufacturing company is its future earnings potential."

So earning potential = intrinsic value. And skills = earning potential.

Tell me again what it is we should invest in.

Credit Cards

Let me share a story. It doesn't pertain to investing, exactly, but it does pertain to having some money in your pocket when you need it.

In the 1960's I married my first wife. Credit cards were just making their debut on the world scene. My parents had never seen a credit card.

At first it was like magic. Too good to be true. To tempting to resist. With a credit card you could buy $100 worth of stuff (a week's salary at that time) and only pay $15 for it. *Per month*, of course. But it was heady stuff and we were inexperienced and didn't know how to handle it. Long story short, after seven years, when my first wife and I split up, we were head over heels in debt.

My second wife and I were married 14 years. And much of that time was spent paying off credit-card debt (both hers and mine). Not to mention student loans. Each time a card was 100% paid off we had a little celebration and destroyed the card. By the time my second wife and I split up, I had zero credit-card debt (which I thought was a great thing) but I had no credit cards either. Which means I didn't have a line of credit (and I didn't realize at the time how serious that could be).

And I lost my job. I was an Industrial Engineering Supervisor working for Alcan Aluminum Corporation. Alcan was headquartered in Montreal. Some 30 years later I chanced to be at a BBQ sitting beside a lady who, as it turned out, actually worked at Alcan headquarters at the very time I lost my job . . . when the decision was made to eliminate all industrial engineering departments (as a cost-saving measure) in all Alcan factories world-wide. As you might imagine, the lady and I had a rather — errr — interesting conversation. (Aside. Alcan was a 1928 spinoff from Alcoa for trust-busting purposes. In 2007 — 79 years later — Alcan was bought out by Rio Tinto for $38 billion.)

But — back in the 80's — there I was. No wife, no job, no income, and no line of credit. I didn't want to leave the area because I was hoping for a reconciliation. But the area (Syracuse, New York) was itself in rather dismal economic straits. GE (dependent on government contracts) and Carrier Air Conditioning were the big local employers and both were struggling at the time. Unemployment was high.

I would interview with somebody. He'd nod approvingly until he glanced down at my résumé and saw what I'd been earning. Then his face would fall. "I'll spend two years training you," he'd say. "But you came from bigger things and you'll return to bigger things. And just about the time you're really earning your keep, local business activity will pick up and you'll be gone. Nope. Can't do it. Sorry."

Over-qualified? It became an old story. The story of me with no money. Unhirable. And no credit cards. Given the fact I didn't have a job — which means I didn't have a source of income — I couldn't *get* a credit card. Playing games was not an option. I couldn't charge some groceries on card #1 and then pay it off with card #2. There was no card #1 or card #2. So, after a few months, the freezer was empty and I was on the verge of losing the house.

Finally I did accept a job offer at a distance and got back in the game. But lesson learned. I accepted every credit card offer that came my way. And, a later on, I insisted that wife #3 do the same. So today we spend a bit of time rotating cards (so they all stay active) and pay them off promptly (so there are no interest charges) but each of us has a credit line over $150K. I probably sleep a little better because of it.

All of us need to invest our assets wisely. And to use our credit wisely. Personally, I think nurturing a high credit limit is a smart move. Just as I thought paying off my house mortgage was a smart move.

Afterword

There is no perfect, foolproof way to preserve wealth. Even the best financial assets can fail. Ditto for barter goods. Even skills can become obsolete. And there are different kinds of people with different needs. And different investing environments.

Consider financial assets. *Stocks?* Every major stock exchange closed for a time during World War I — New York for five months; both Berlin (Germany) and St. Petersburgh (Russia) for three years. *Land?* In Russia, land was confiscated by the soviets in 1917. *Gold?* Gold was confiscated by the U.S. government in 1933. *Bitcoin?* Crypto was outlawed by China in 2021.

Frank Leslie's Illustrated Newspaper from 1873 has a cover picture (a wood engraving) with a caption that reads, "The Great Financial Panic of 1873 — Closing the door of the [New York] Stock Exchange on its members, Saturday, Sept. 20th." It shows a mob of pushing, shoving men dressed in suits and high hats. From 1873? One might conclude that financial panics and stock exchange closings are not exactly new. https://www.loc.gov/resource/cph.3a37787/

Consider barter goods. *Flashlight batteries?* I've returned for refund Duracell AA batteries after two years (although guaranteed for 10 years) because they were heavily corroded. Brand new. Still in the unopened package.

Consider skills. Knowing how to use a treadle sewing machine would be fantastic if the grid went down. That's how my mother (and both grandmothers) made clothes for the whole family. But do you, or does anyone you know, own a treadle machine today? In working condition?

And there are all kinds of people with different needs. Young and old. Rich and poor. Healthy and sick. And every combination thereof.

And different environments. Is it wartime or peace? Dictatorship or democracy? Are you a baby boomer approaching end-of-life? Or are you young enough that you'll still be around when the boomers have expired?

Time for a story.

When I worked in Toronto I rented an apartment and became close friends with the landlord (a man whom we'll call Ryan). Ryan — a millionaire kinda guy — hailed from India.

Ryan bought a summer camp and my wife and I spent many pleasant weekends there with Ryan and his wife. The camp developed a roof leak. I looked at it. Told Ryan what I thought needed to be done. Then I accompanied Ryan into town to get the necessary supplies. It was our discussion on the way to town that stuck in my mind.

Ryan understood that to me (a white male from upstate New York), knowing how to "do things" was a source of pride. A source of bragging rights. Yes, Ryan, I know how to change the oil in a car. I've done it. And, yes, I know how to change the *engine* in a car. My friends and I did that as teenagers. The more things you know how to do — butcher a pig, turn threads on a metal lathe, saddle a horse — the more manly you're entitled to feel about yourself.

So what Ryan then said in reply astounded me. In India, he informed me, your biggest bragging rights come from *not* knowing how to do *anything*. India was once a caste society. Even today, the super-rich know how to do *nothing* and are proud of it. Knowing how to "do" something would be an admission that you're not really super-rich. So you make an effort to remain ignorant. Ignorance is a status symbol.

Actually there was a third man in the car with us on our ride to town. Another Indian chap. And he nodded his head — continuously — in agreement with what Ryan was telling me.

Say what? Our talk left my head spinning. But we did get the roof fixed.

Also in Toronto, my wife had a lady friend who had emigrated from the Philippines and married a man who had emigrated from Germany. The lady laughs about it today, telling how, when she was first married, she didn't know how to change a light bulb. She came from a well-to-do family and servants had always done such things for her. She sat on the edge of the bed and cried tears when her new husband *insisted* that she herself change the bulb.

The point to all this?

Cultural upbringing notwithstanding, from a survivalist standpoint you need to know how to "do" things (drive a standard-shift car, sharpen a knife, bake bread, etc.). And the world is changing; you need to put down your cell phone occasionally and read the news and keep abreast of world developments. You need to diversify your investments. You need to save some of your money and not spend all of it. You need to avoid debt. You need to stay healthy. You need to get right with your fellow man. That's a big one.

Money and gold and crypto will only take you so far. And knowing how to do things will only take you so far. Having *friends* is the real bottom line. Granted, money and knowledge and skills all make life easier. But you still need emotional validation. You still need someone to reach out and grab your shoulder when you wobble on your crutches.

We all hit streaks of bad luck from time to time — financially, health-wise, love-wise. It's built into the nature of things. And when those hard times arrive, there's an old saying that sums it up quite nicely: "You're only as strong as your friends are." We should never forget that.

About the Author

This is the author's bio that appears on the Amazon Kindle page.
https://www.amazon.com/Ron-Brown/e/B08LB1R7L8/ref=aufs_dp_fta_dsk

GAYE LEVY: Let us start out by learning a little bit about you. Tell us about yourself and how you ended up where you are today.

RON BROWN: Born 1940. Attended a one-room schoolhouse. Had a pony as a child and a horse as a teenager. Graduated college on the dean's list.

Speaking of genealogy, I joined The Sons of the American Revolution in my 20's. Married 3 times. Delivered 2 babies at home. My second wife and I had a "his, hers, and ours" marriage with custody of — gulp! — 11 children.

At 42 I published my first magazine article in the magazine *Countryside*. Heated with firewood most of my life in addition to raising a vegetable garden and livestock. Third wife is from the Philippines. She and I taught country-western dancing in the 90's.

Worked as an industrial engineering supervisor, production control supervisor, and consultant. Retired at 62 and began collecting Social Security but received a job offer I couldn't refuse in Canada.

Finally, at 65, I *really* retired.

GAYE LEVY: After retirement, but before this book — *Prepper's Guide to Wealth* — you wrote a series of books on non-electric lighting. What was that all about?

RON BROWN: When I began working in Canada (August 1, 2003), the company put us up for three months in a furnished luxury townhouse (bedding on the beds, dishes in the cupboards, pool, maid service, all that). They wanted us to hit the ground running and not fret about trivial things like housing. As a consequence, we brought no preps with us.

Two weeks later (August 14) the lights went out in the entire northeast for several days. We had no food in the cupboard, no Canadian money, and not so much as one candle for lighting. When the sun went down it got dark.

Later on my wife confessed, "You don't know how close I was to begging you — I'm scared. I don't care about the job. I don't care about the money. Let's go home." (I never told her there wasn't enough gas in the car to get back to the border.)

That blackout was the impetus for the eight-book Non-Electric Lighting Series. It's been well received. Today, whenever I feel sorry for myself, I go to Amazon and browse the reader feedback. Gee, maybe I'm not such a bad guy after all.

About Gaye Levy (author of the Foreword):

Gaye Levy grew up and attended school in the Greater Seattle area. After spending many years as an executive in the software industry. She abandoned city life and moved to an offshore island in Washington State then later to the mountain Rim Country of Arizona.

For many years Gaye was a blogger where she taught the principles of a sustainable and self-reliant lifestyle through her former website, *Backdoor Survival*. Now retired, she still blogs from time to time at the *Strategic Living Blog*.

Prepping and survival are a big part of Gaye's life and she is proud to consider herself a "maker" and a do-er, utilizing her skills and learning new ones on a daily basis.

To read more from Gaye, visit her website, *Strategic Living*. You can purchase her eBook, *Prepper's Guide to Food Storage* on Amazon.com.

Other Books by Ron Brown

The Non-Electric Lighting Series is available on Amazon in both Kindle e-book and paperback format.

- **Book 1: Candles**

  ". . . a joy to read. I had found my mother's candle-making supplies and now have some idea what to do with them . . . just straightforward, basic information. Thank you, Mr. Brown." — Amazon Customer

- **Book 2: Olive Oil Lamps &c.**

  "Very informative and interesting . . . A must-have for the modern prepper . . . I consider it a great value. The pictures are clear and the descriptions . . . are excellent." — Moss VanGogh

- **Book 3: Lamp Fuels**

  "Absolutely a MUST READ for anyone using non-electric lighting . . . enough talk. Just GET THIS BOOK!" — totallyfrozen

- **Book 4: Kerosene Lamps**

  "Five Stars. Everything I expected and more!" — NE

- **Book 5: Coleman Gas Lanterns**

  "Yabadabadoo! Read it from cover to cover upon receipt. Great info, perspective, and writing style." — Brian Swift

- **Book 6: Kerosene Pressure Lanterns**

  "I learned more about kerosene pressure lanterns in 30 minutes with this book than anyone ever told me and more than I'd learned in hours of watching YouTube . . . I highly recommend this book and the other books in the series." — totallyfrozen

- **Book 7: Propane for Preppers**

  "Outstanding article! One of the BEST I've ever read or seen on any preparedness website." — TPS

  [Much of the material in Book 7 originally appeared as a series of five articles in the prepper's blog *Backdoor Survival*.]

- **Book 8: Alcohol Mantle Lamps**

  "Best in the series. Rare and stellar information." — John Decatur

- **The Amazing 2000-Hour Flashlight**

  "Perfect." — Virginia Candela

- **The New 2000-Hour Flashlight**

  "This is a wonderful book. Kudos to Ron Brown." — Brian R

- There's also a (free) YouTube video entitled **"Converting a Gas Lantern to Kerosene."**

  "Ron, your instructions, organization, and style are the best I have seen anywhere. If you aren't doing instructional videos for a living, you should." — Guiding Mike

Printed in Great Britain
by Amazon

19685991R00068